ADIRONDACK
REFLECTIONS

ADIRONDACK
REFLECTIONS

On Life and Living in the Mountains and the Valleys

Edited by Neal Burdick and Maurice Kenny

THE
History
PRESS

Published by The History Press
Charleston, SC 29403
www.historypress.net

Front cover: top, David Pynchon; middle, Tara Freeman; bottom, Debbie Kanze.
Back cover: inset, Jean Williams-Bergen; top, Henning Vahlenkamp; bottom, Barry Lobdell.

First published 2013

Manufactured in the United States

ISBN 978.1.62619.116.7

Library of Congress CIP data applied for.

CONTENTS

CONTENTS

FOREWORD

Here's what I like about this book: it is unabashedly about this place, *these* Adirondacks. No excuses, like "the stories could happen anywhere," or "this is not a work by simply regional writers"—you get the idea. The editors, to their credit, are not ashamed that this volume is about a very specific place and very specific people. It may be true that you could read—and like—this collection on a ranch in Wyoming or in a Manhattan condo, but the book is about *our* place, right here in the Adirondacks and the North Country.

If you've lived here—or visited the region with any regularity—each of these essays will get the bells ringing for you, about wood-splitting or hiking, hobby farms and rural poverty. Some will take you a bit beyond the familiar bells, as Lita Kelly does with her reminiscence about the presence of prisons in many communities—a fact of Adirondack life usually overlooked.

I want to upgrade my language: I love this book. It brings together essays by some of our best writers—many of whom I've followed for years, a few I've just met with real delight—all focusing on us, on our place, on this scrabbly rocky bit of ground we drilled our roots into.

Put this book on your nightstand, first. Then move it to the coffee table. Next to the counter in your kitchen, where you perch on a stool while the teakettle water comes to a boil. Keep it moving around the house. Everyone will pick it up and dip in where the bell rings for them.

ELLEN ROCCO
North Country Public Radio
Winter 2013

INTRODUCTION

There was a time when this volume and its twin, *North Country Reflections*, were to be one book, with the title *Being: North*. We both felt those two words captured the fact that people live and work, dream and play, suffer and endure—in other words, *exist*—"up here" and captured the essence of where "here" is. But projects grow and evolve when they acquire momentum, and this one expanded in both scope and name.

For a great many years, those who wrote about the region that is the focus of these books were few in number, and they mostly lived elsewhere, only visiting or passing through before retreating to the relative comforts of more urban (and urbane) environments when the weather turned cold and the income grew slim. But beginning with the last quarter of the twentieth century, the region has seen an outpouring of place-based writing by both old hands and newcomers, most of whom have chosen to take up residence, preferring the subtle and often hidden advantages of living in the mountains and rural expanses to the heavily trumpeted disadvantages. It is those writers, some of whom have never been published before, to whom we wished to offer a platform with these books. Aside from the fact that we want you to discover them, we also want them to discover each other.

Many people helped bring these books into being. Foremost among them, of course, are the more than three dozen contributors of written and artistic works. We thank them for sharing their creative talents, for giving of their energy and, above all, for their patience. Special accolades go to Tara Freeman, staff photographer at St. Lawrence University, for her priceless technical assistance with the images.

Whether you label it the North Country or the Adirondacks or some combination of the two, the misshapen chunk of New York State that protrudes northward from Interstate 90, beyond the northernmost mainline of American east–west commerce, is a special place in its own special ways. We hope these two books help you come to understand, appreciate and wonder about it a little more.

NEAL BURDICK
MAURICE KENNY
Mud Season, 2013

Part I
The Land

THE PLEASURES OF LOWLAND HIKING

By Rich Frost

It's a bit unclear in my memory which of us was more devastated when Furry couldn't finish the climb up Debar Mountain.

Furry, our fourteen-year-old black Lab, had been our companion on so many hikes that it never occurred to me that a day would come when she couldn't climb anymore. She'd been with us atop Pok-o-Moonshine and Gilligan, Baxter and Goodnow, Cascade and Big Slide. At times when my wife and I began dragging, Furry could always provide the extra encouragement necessary to reach the top.

Naturally, I considered the Debar experience just an aberration. So Furry came along on our next outing to Hurricane. Again, she faltered before achieving her goal. When we left to climb Hopkins a couple weeks later, we decided to leave her home.

Her look of disappointment—could it be one of betrayal?—burned itself into my consciousness. I knew I couldn't bear looking at that face every time I left on a hike.

And that's when we learned how much more there is to Adirondack hiking than bagging peaks.

We took out the guidebooks and began the search for more modest trails. After all, there are valleys in between all those mountains. There are relentlessly coursing rivers. Courtesy of the last ice age, there's no shortage of remote ponds and lakes. Courtesy of early settlers, there's a host of abandoned roads.

Consequently we found enjoyment in reaching the Hudson River gorge at the end of the Blue Ledges trail. An afternoon trekking Old Ironville Road reminded us of the way people had to get from place to place in an earlier era.

The Moriah ponds and the Hammond Pond Wild Forest became especially valuable resources. Short trails brought us to Crowfoot Pond and Berrymill Flow. Twice when Furry seemed somewhat more energetic, we continued on from Berrymill to Moose Mountain Pond.

The Boreas River Trail, however, was the one that cemented our newly gained appreciation of what I'll call the lowland Adirondacks. Like Norman MacLean, who wrote *A River Runs Through It*, I'm a bit haunted by waters. It's still a source of amazement and wonder how the flow of a river constantly renews itself as it courses to its outlet. Springtime thaws are easily understood as sources of water; the springs that keep streams full are more elusive.

In reading of the Boreas, we learned how it served as one of the public highways open to all comers during the heyday of the logging industry. Walking along, we tried to imagine the sight of this waterway choked with logs.

About a mile into our hike, I spotted an iron ring bolted to a large rock. My imagination took me back to river-driving days. I conjured up images of men in wool shirts and calked shoes maneuvering atop rolling logs branded with company names. I saw them breaking up jams with pike poles. I had a hazy vision of some falling into the water and drowning.

Our change in focus allowed Furry to hike another two years. Her last outing was a mere month or so before she died at age sixteen.

Fast-forward a few years. Ripken is now the reigning canine monarch around our homestead. He's just twelve, but a spinal cord injury forced a premature end to his North Country climbing days. This time we have no reason to watch his disappointment at being left behind for an ascent of, say, Wright Peak or Phelps. Rather we ourselves savor the chance to go back to a regimen of less steep hiking.

We've gone back to Boreas River, where that iron ring is harder to find because of the enveloping foliage, but it's still there. Ripken loves the chance to wade near Rocky Falls, along the Indian Pass Trail. Taking our time, we've enjoyed a satisfying fall excursion down the broad wagon path to Camp Santanoni.

One fall morning I had an urge to find an abandoned graphite mine in the Putnam Pond area. My wife was skeptical, but Ripken left no doubt he was game. We'd never hiked in this area before, but topographic maps indicated there would be no prolonged steep stretches.

Keeping our eyes open to natural oddities, we were rewarded with a glimpse of a circumferential burl around one tree, the largest burl I've ever seen. Ripken, on the other hand, kept alert to the presence of water. He was well rewarded on this particular trip, having the chance to frolic in Putnam,

North, Heart and Rock Ponds. His hips may have become problematic, but that had no impact on his ability to swim.

By Rock Pond, seemingly in the midst of nowhere, we found our destination. A mine shaft cut into the hillside leaked out a trickle of brown water. Stone wall remnants testified to what must have once been a multistory building. Nearby rested a metal boiler, the circumference of which matched our heights.

Certainly there must have been a road to this spot at one time, but we couldn't detect any evidence. Had we searched more diligently, would we have discovered foundations of boardinghouses? Or did men (I doubt there were women) come to the mine daily from nearby settlements? One of these days, I'll scrutinize old maps and try to determine who owned this company and how they got their product to market.

Completely uninterested in these historical ruminations, Ripken had begun swimming laps in Rock Pond. If he rued the loss of opportunity to climb more high peaks, he certainly didn't let on.

Is there any lesson in all this?

Well, our dogs have forced on us a deeper and broader appreciation of the Adirondacks. What we've found on our lowland hikes sends us to old maps and countless history books to learn more about the human forces that have interacted with the forests, mountains and waterways. Such activity has also enticed us to learn more geology, with special attention to how ice once carved this landscape.

Furry and Ripken have also shown us that one need never lose that verve for life. They taught us also the necessity for—and the satisfactions of— adaptation. Inability to scale high peaks didn't consign them to an indoor life; rather, it opened a marvelous new arena for exploration.

I'm about eight dog years old myself now. When my days of climbing end, I won't be languishing in defeat. Instead I'll be welcoming an opportunity to add to my Adirondack repertoire.

Sure, I'll miss the dramatic views should the time come when I can't reach a mountain top lookout. (In fairness, I keep Belfry Mountain in reserve, its fire tower accessible by a mere half-mile walk up the fire observer's road.) And I'll miss that quest to become an Adirondack 46er—one who has climbed all forty-six peaks thought at one time to be over four thousand feet in altitude—though my progress along those lines has been slow anyway. That doesn't mean, however, that I'll be missing scenes of remarkable beauty or cheating myself of memorable destinations.

People from afar know this region as the "Adirondack Mountains." Courtesy of our canine companions, we know that's just the beginning.

WE CAME, WE STAYED: BUILDING AN ADIRONDACK LIFE

By Edward Kanze

W hen killing frosts descended on our tomato plants during our first Adirondack July, we knew we were in for a challenge. And the following winter, when eighteen feet of snow fell on our eighteen and a half acres and I had to shovel the roofs of the house and shed weekly to stave off collapse, the dimensions of the challenge began to come clear. We got in the habit of hauling tarps over the vegetable garden that summer. Every gorgeous but pitiless starry night when the temperature outside fell to forty degrees Fahrenheit by bedtime, we covered. And when snow from the roof piled up around the back of the house as high as the eaves, I carved holes through the banks (banks so high I no longer needed a ladder to reach the roof) to allow light in and us to gaze out.

Theodore Roosevelt championed the "strenuous life." My wife, Debbie, and I looked at each other and, without saying a word, knew that this was it.

At age thirty-nine and forty-two, she and I had moved to Saranac Lake, a bustling village of three thousand just north of the Adirondack High Peaks, in the last year of the old millennium. Most recently, we'd been living on the Maine coast and working as rangers at Acadia National Park. We'd been migrant workers for the National Park Service on and off for years, working seasonally at Gulf Islands National Seashore in Mississippi and Great Smoky Mountains National Park in Tennessee before coming to Maine. In the middle of it all, we squeezed in a year-long camping trip in Australia and New Zealand, followed a bit later by a year and a half in Ithaca, New York.

But the gypsy life was wearing thin. We were ready to settle down. At least, we thought we were.

When we arrived, we were homeless. A significant proportion of our worldly possessions was crammed into a rusting, badly overloaded Toyota station wagon with 150,000 miles on the ticker.

Dear friends had offered us use of a cabin at the end of a dead-end road in Keene Valley. The structure, casually insulated, came with a good woodstove and an empty woodshed. We arrived on one of the last golden afternoons of September; nighttime temperatures were regularly plunging below freezing. I quickly got to work with a chainsaw, putting up some stump-dried birch, beech and maple in the shed.

Other aspects of our original Adirondack domestic arrangements brought greater challenges. We had no running water, which meant no toilet and no water for drinking or brushing teeth except what we carried from the village in jugs. An early chore was digging a pit privy. It had to be far enough from the cabin and a nearby stream to be private, safe and legal, yet close enough for comfort and convenience on cold dark nights. The fact that bears inhabited the woods in considerable number made after-hours use of our sanitary system exciting. To complete the set-up, we drove a forked stick into the ground, hung a roll of toilet paper on it and sheltered the paper from the elements in a plastic bag.

Because Debbie would be looking for a job, and because we both hoped to socialize with our new neighbors a bit, a way to bathe had to be devised. We could have used the kind of old-fashioned hip bath you see in westerns, where a tired cowboy immerses his private parts in hot water in a small tub, legs hanging out one end and upper body sticking out the top. Lacking such a modern convenience, however, we simply stood in front of the woodstove on a towel and scrubbed with a washcloth dunked in warm soapy water. Shampooing was done over the kitchen sink.

I'd be giving a false impression of our fortitude if I failed to report a happy development that came our second week. At the then-bustling Keene Valley Bookstore, we'd met a woman named Constance Miller. She was one of Keene Valley's grand dames, a pillar of the local Republican party, and she lived at a nearby camp, a fine old place with the unforgettable name "Mossy Casserole." Constance looked aghast upon hearing of our mode of living. She took particular pity on Debbie, I think, which accounts for the invitation we received to her house for twice-weekly hot showers. The fact that the showers were followed by gin and tonics, Constance's marvelous conversation and, often, a home-cooked meal had much to do with a brightening of our morale. She invited us to enjoy her washer and dryer, too.

Within a day or two of arriving, we climbed into the car one morning and drove to Bloomingdale, six miles north and east of Saranac Lake. We had an appointment to keep. Sandy Hayes, a Bloomingdale real estate agent, had been the only Adirondack representative of his profession kind or forgiving enough to return Debbie's letters from Maine. She'd written to a half dozen or so agents, spelling out what we were looking for and giving a sense of our puny budget. Others hadn't bothered to respond, but Sandy was friendly and eager.

His efforts were rewarded, as it turned out. The first place he showed us made our stomachs churn. It was, on one hand, the worst house we'd ever visited as potential buyers. The one-story wooden structure had bits of charm here and there in the interior, but the roof leaked, the exterior walls begged for painting, the floor joists were badly rotted, the beams that held up the joists had rotted away, the foundation was broken and twisted in places, the wiring needed to be replaced, the plumbing needed the same and the whole structure was filled with mouse droppings. Worse yet, the place had been built for summer use only. The walls were uninsulated, the water pipes were exposed, the house had no heating system and water arrived via a jet pump on the surface a couple hundred feet from the foundation wall and a line buried only a few inches deep—not deep enough, not by a long shot, to safely convey water to the house in winter.

On the other hand, our stomachs churned because this nightmare of a structure was beautifully situated on a low hill overlooking a quiet bend of the Saranac River. Five or six acres of lawn surrounded the house, lawn that we'd turn feral and hand over to the goldenrods and garter snakes if we had the chance. The property also included two acres directly across the river and another ten acres or so on the far side of the road. The road was just the kind we'd decided long ago we wanted to live on. It went nowhere, or to put it another way, it dead-ended. To give a better sense of our perspective, it led just where we most wanted to go: into the heart of the adjacent McKenzie Mountain Wilderness Area. (The pavement ended at the last of the handful of houses scattered along our road, and beyond, a dirt road continued another mile until it became a boat ramp and plunged into the north end of a deep lake. Grand views of Whiteface, Moose and McKenzie Mountains opened to the south and east.) All the land visible from the house either came with the property title or fell within the state forest preserve, the latter protected as "forever wild" according to the New York State Constitution.

At the same time, the house and property lay a mere two miles from the nearest grocery store and post office. If the car broke down—always a possibility given the kind of cars we tended to drive—we could bike, walk or snowshoe. The village of Saranac Lake, a possible source of jobs and certain source of social contact, loomed eight flat, easily pedaled miles down the road. Saranac Lake, among its long list of virtues as a potential home place, included a year-round professional theater, an institution not quite up to Broadway standards but offering impressive productions of plays ranging from Shakespeare to Shaw to a miscellany of musicals, comedy and melodrama. Lake Placid, nine miles away, offered winter sports and a Center for the Arts that screened the latest highbrow foreign films (albeit months behind Manhattan) and staged a fabulous potpourri of music and ballet.

Debbie and I could both glimpse the future. If we bought the place, we'd spend the next decade of our lives reclaiming a structure that the contractor we hired to evaluate it advised us to bulldoze. Yet we'd also find ourselves living in an environment of surpassing richness: one with a beautiful wild river flowing past our doorstep, with all its associated frogs, salamanders, birds, beavers, otters, mosquitoes, blackflies and no-see-ums; one with a magnificent lake we could walk to just down the road; one with no neighbors we could see but rather neighbors tucked conveniently out of sight in both directions; one with culture available just around the corner and enough economic infrastructure to hold the promise of jobs.

Optimism won out over despair. We bought the place. Now let's jump ahead a decade.

We're still here. Surely Sandy Hayes and a good many others must have been surprised to see us weather the storms of progress. With our friend Tom LeBaron, a contractor, guiding us and providing hard labor, we sluiced concrete into the dark, filthy crawl space, poured it into wooden forms, slid in new beams (paid for by an old college friend and his wife who sent a check in a not-so-random act of kindness), jacked the beams off the concrete after it had cured and hammered in new floor joists.

Much of the labor and nearly all of the encouragement came from a pair of brothers, James and John Junker. The three of us have known each other and remained close friends since I was three years old. My parents were downstate neighbors and close friends of their parents, and through the parental grapevine, James and John had learned that Debbie and I were floundering. So one day they appeared in a van stuffed with building materials and tools. For nine days they worked, from seven or eight every morning until nine o'clock at night (except for one day, when we kept going until midnight). They had taken time off from their jobs, one of them without pay, and from us they would accept nothing more than food and drink. The episode provided a solemn lesson in the beauty and value of friendship. Without it, we might have frozen to death or been crushed under a heap of snow.

While any of us might fancy himself, or herself, the rugged independent sort who pulls his hindquarters up by his bootstraps, the truth is, all progress, including ours, flows from the contributions of many tributaries. In addition to the Junker brothers, contributions in the form of money, materials and cheer came from parents and late grandparents, from generous aunts and kind uncles, from supportive siblings and dear generous friends. Slowly, beginning in the crawl space and rising upward, a new house began to take shape from the old. Faulty wiring and plumbing were ripped out and replaced; a new submersible pump was dropped into our 117-foot deep well (I measured the depth myself with bits of teabag string that, in a playful experiment in frugality, I'd saved and knotted together); a six-foot-deep trench was dug by a backhoe to convey water through a frost-free line to the house; and a plugged pipe to the septic tank was diagnosed, unearthed and repaired. In terms of backbreaking effort, I'll never forget the day James and I spent hand-digging the trench for the water line under eight feet of porch and under a foundation wall. The trench had to be six feet deep. The stony soil we displaced might have filled a dozen bathtubs.

I could fill more than a tub with stories of our horror and success. Suffice it to say that we completed the most onerous tasks within the first year, and while projects will always loom over our heads like rain clouds, we soon began enjoying our new surroundings.

We fell in love with the community, biological and cultural, and I like to think that the community—the human one, for one can never be sure of the feelings of muskrats and maple trees—developed a fondness for us. Debbie quickly found one job and then another. The second proved congenial beyond her dreams: serving as activities director at Saranac Village at Will Rogers, a "senior independent living residence," as they're known in the trade. She puts together a busy schedule of concerts, games, lectures, performances and birthday parties, and her field trips range as far as Glens Falls, Watertown, Burlington and Montreal. Once I helped her escort a group of spirited seniors to a Montreal Expos night game.

As for me, I spent my first couple years as an Adirondack homeowner saving our home from ruin. With Debbie working alongside on evenings and weekends, I soldered, glued, sawed, planed, hammered, hung, taped, replaced, wired, insulated, caulked, weather-stripped and patched. I installed a pricey, top-of-the-line metal chimney and connected it to a woodstove and then spent much of the winter out in the woods with a chainsaw, felling black cherry trees that a disease called black knot had destroyed. I carried the logs on snowshoes back to the house, one heavy armload at a time. Many a moonlit night I was out there in the snow, and Debbie sometimes, too, fetching firewood at one o'clock in the morning.

Through it all I was writing newspaper columns and magazine features and, for a few months, running a small not-for-profit organization promoting Adirondack writing and writers. But the house, the eighteen acres, the woodstove and their incessant demands made it impossible to spare the energy the writing group deserved. So I handed over the tiller to a successor and marched back into the salt mine.

A couple years later, years during which I promoted a newly published travel book I'd written about Australia and begun work on a novel, I was driving to a dental appointment in Lake Placid one morning when a tire blew out on the front of the car. It was a new tire, installed incorrectly the day before. The car, a "new" old rusty station wagon we'd just purchased, surely had a jack hiding inside it somewhere, but I couldn't find the thing. What to do? Lacking a cell phone, I knocked on the nearest door.

I've forgotten what played out in the dentist's chair when I eventually arrived, but the conversation I had with the man who let me call a taxi remains fresh. He was Joe Hackett, a legendary Adirondack guide. We talked while I waited. In the course of things it came out that I had a quarter century's experience leading nature walks for national parks, state parks, county parks and nature centers, and I had just launched a small guiding business of my own. I confessed I had little work. Joe confessed he had too much. He generously offered to introduce me around at legendary Adirondack establishments such as the Point on Upper Saranac Lake and the Lake Placid Lodge. In short order, I was guiding guests of these places and others, too. Thanks in large part to Joe, my business gained critical momentum.

Around the same time, as Debbie and I edged into our mid-forties, a wild notion came into our heads. How about kids? We'd always loved children, other people's children, the kind that leave you exhausted but go back where they came from after a few hours, yet we had never actively entertained the notion of producing some of our own. Now, with the window of opportunity poised to slam closed on us, we found ourselves living in a dreamy place for kids. Should we? Could we? Most importantly, would we?

I am delighted and, in hindsight, immensely relieved to say that we decided to give conception a chance. There were a couple of false starts, including a heartbreaking one where Debbie heard a fetal heartbeat at the doctor's office. A couple days later, I held Debbie's hand during an ultrasound exam. She was ready to share the excitement with me, but instead of excitement, there came grief. Happily, the third time was the charm. Baby Ned (Edward IV) was born after forty-two hours of intermittent labor when Debbie was forty-three and I nearly forty-seven. A baby sister, Tassie (Tasman Victoria), followed not quite two years later.

I like to say, and like to think, that our kids exist because of the marvelous place where we live. It's true, although only a partial truth. No doubt our kids also exist because we love each other and because we love our parents and loved our grandparents and rejoice in perpetuating their genes. We love aunts and uncles and siblings and our community and our neighbors, too. I know: it all sounds sappy. But every word is true. In the early weeks of cradling babies, it struck me that I'd become a gushing hydrant of love. Love of life and love of family and love of just about everything poured from me in a torrent at all hours, even when I had to change a diaper or mop up vomit at a cruel hour. Sure, I complained, loudly. But mostly I felt liberated. I had given away my free will (if indeed I ever really had any) and surrendered myself body and soul to universal forces. If, as biologists argue, our very beings consist of little more than mechanisms for the propagation of genes, then, by golly, it felt grand to be a mechanism. Yahoo! I was euphoric to be a parent—a father with crow's feet fanning out from his eyes and gray hair multiplying as I neared my fiftieth birthday.

I still feel that way. I feel that way about the kids, about the place, about the neighbors. I am lucky to be here in this time and place with this wife and these children amid these beautiful and biologically diverse mountains and these rugged, idiosyncratic neighbors. In one way or another, we're all here because we want to be here, because we choose the cold of the North Country over the easy warmth of Florida, the bear and bobcats and biting insects over the biologically impoverished suburbs. Life is often hard here in our corner of the North Country. Yet it's rich beyond imagining.

FROM WASTELAND TO WILDERNESS

By Alan L. Steinberg

He found him in a desert land, and in the howling waste of the wilderness; He encircled him, He cared for him, He kept him as the apple of His eye.
—*Deuteronomy 32:9–10 RSV*

The pastures of the wilderness drip, the hills gird themselves with joy, the meadows clothe themselves with flocks, the valleys deck themselves with grain, they shout and sing together for joy.
—*Psalm 65:9-13 RSV*

I want to tell you a story about wilderness. It begins in Brooklyn, in Bedford-Stuyvesant—a strange place to begin, I know. My mother brought me there. She remarried, and the man she married lived there, ran a store there. She left another part of Brooklyn to move there, but that doesn't really matter. There were a few more trees where she had lived, where I had been born. More gardens, perhaps. Though what I remember most even there were the schoolyards, the concrete fields that taught us how tough life could be—though not as tough and hardscrabble and raw as in Bed-Stuy.

It was during the sixties and Bedford-Stuyvesant was a powder keg of grievances—some racial, some economic, some religious, some political. But mostly, Bed-Stuy was urban—urban in a fierce way. By that I mean it was urban in its consciousness, in its rhythms, in its arrogance, in its decay. It was as if the earth had always been brick and pavement, curb and street, fluorescent and neon. There was never darkness. Never a night sky so free of human incandescence you could see more than a handful of the billion stars flickering there. There was never quiet. Never a natural sound that once begun could die out on its own without interruption, without being drowned or shattered or pierced by the human sounds of motors, of sirens, of laughter, of screams.

And what passed for wilderness, at least for me, was wasteland. Empty lots. Deserted parks. Fenced and wired yards. Narrow alleys clotted with garbage cans and papers and bottles and hypodermic needles. And solitude—that serene sense that you're standing alert and alone with all of eternity stretched out before you—was only the uneasy feeling that comes with walking in fog and shadow, with not quite being able to make out the shifting shapes and sounds closing in around you. Solitude meant isolation, and isolation was dangerous. You couldn't spend much time looking at what lay before you when you were always worrying about what was coming up behind you. Was that only a stunted tree's twisted shadow, or a mugger, or a druggie, or something worse? In its own perverse way, then, what passed for wilderness in the city made you more self-conscious rather than less; made you feel more confined rather than free; pushed you more into yourself rather than let you drift, easy and flowing, into the universe. Or so it seemed to me back then, living one brick wall away from a dying urban hospital and rows of rusted, gated, barred and graffitied brownstone buildings.

For me, then, in those years of growing up in Brooklyn, the wilderness, the natural world, was more like the Waste Land of Eliot's poem—more like the wasteland of the Old Testament, which it echoed—a place cursed by God to be barren, harsh and unyielding, where Cain, brother-less and abandoned, feared every shadow and clap of thunder.

And then a kind of miracle happened. By dint of technical poverty and fortuitous extended family connections, I was given a place in an Adirondack charity-camp: two weeks in the mountains, by a lake you could walk in and swim in and fish in; surrounded by acres and acres of fields and meadows that beguiled you with the smells of wildflowers of every shape and hue and bedeviled you with the buzz and whine and bite of a million insects all conspiring to drive you inside or mad. But I was tough, and so were my bunkmates and campmates. And for all the mosquitoes and wasps and poison ivy and sumac, Eliot's "wasteland" turned into London's "call of the wild." Warnings about bears and coyotes and foxes and skunks meant nothing to us. Did they carry guns? Knives? Crack and pot?

Mark Twain once said he got religious only at night. That first dark night by the campfired lake I knew exactly what he meant, what Keats had meant a century before when he had written

then on the shore
Of the wide world I stand alone, and think
Till love and fame to nothingness do sink.

Stars filled the ebony sky, shimmered on the water like sapphires on a velvet gown. There was the lap of water against the shore, against the wooden dock, against the aluminum boats, against our urban souls. There was cricket-cry and owl-cry and beetle-click and toad-croak.

For two weeks, we went up into those mountains; up curling dirt paths that wound round and round like swirls of chocolate on a vanilla cone and brought us to ledges and clearings that let us gaze on fat-bellied meadows and tree-bald clearings and blue-eyed ponds and brown-veined streams. There were eagles and hawks and blackbirds and crows floating like kites in the cloud-plush air. And bushes everywhere, filled with berries we were warned not to eat and stumps and rocks and tree crotches sprouting spoors and mushrooms and lime-green lichens. And every so often, like an oasis in the Biblical desert, there would be prickly bushes of blackberries or raspberries and tangled masses of tiny lush-ripe strawberries that made the store-bought kind taste like cardboard.

In one fell swoop—in one mere fortnight—I had gone from wasteland-fearing urbanite to wilderness-seeking dreamer. The scales had fallen from my eyes. All those poets I had read, with their dream-talk of woodlands and meadows, and all those Biblical prayers I had chanted giving thanks for the gifts of myrrh and myrtle and mandrake suddenly became real to me. Not just syllables on a page, but a catalog of wonders, a recipe for right living.

As Chaucer had written centuries ago, my world was turned "upside down." My life in the city that had seemed so essential, so foundational, so consequential now seemed strangely artificial. Standing under such a big sky, under such steep and jagged mountains, under such thick and towering trees made the cramped and crumbling brownstone and brick buildings of Brooklyn seem so ordinary and plain. I didn't know it then, but one day my road would lead out of the concrete city and into that same world of big sky and mountain—first to Washington and then to Oregon and then to Idaho, before it would lead back east and into those very same Adirondacks that made both my skin and soul shiver.

For more than twenty years now, I have lived in the North Country. The sky is still a wonder. The Adirondacks, laminated with icy snow, still seem big, even after years of hiking the Sawtooths and Tetons. The cold is long and unapologetic and sometimes makes it difficult and dangerous to linger.

The meadows and fields are still larded with berries and bugs—little bugs, little black and biting bugs. And there is quiet—not silence, but the balanced harmony of the earth breathing in and breathing out, giving life and a melancholy joy to all the living things passing through and not passing by.

Let me end my story with a poem, one not written by a native but by one born in Brooklyn, one who came to the North Country and was lucky enough to stay:

Adirondack Spring

Sun finds him
wet and cold
in the last snow
of winter,
the bitter snow,
the black snow,
the snow that shatters
on the humpbacked ground.

The air which scraped
his spirit raw
grows soft and tender,
light with light
and the scent of green.
He feels a charity
well within,
forgives the gods
that brought him here,
that made the cold
and this last black snow
to break him.

WINTER BLUES AND DARKNESS: LOST AND FOUND

By Jennifer Duffield White

I'm feeling bold. I have a theory; I have a plan.

Once upon a time, I think I chomped through the days of winter with relative youthful ease. Last winter, though, I had a rough go of it. I hesitated. I lay in bed for long hours. I got soft and slow.

For the record, I love snow, the four seasons, the descent into winter. But last year I surfaced into spring knowing the weight of winter in the mental sense, in the lost-frozen-breath sense. Part of it I blamed on other things—work, health and otherwise. Even my doctor complained about the high percentage of cloudy days that winter as I lay stretched out on an exam table while he sliced out my history with the sun. This winter, he's still giving me scars; I'm still rocking in front of the picture window each morning, bathing in a stream of chilled sunlight.

But I'm executing the plan.

No gym membership this year. For many years, I thought the companionship of other sweaty souls running in place on machines while staring at a television was my solution to winter loneliness and fitness. Gym memberships are not my savior.

The darkness, I have decided, is my friend. Instead of uncorking a bottle of wine with the setting of the sun, I strap on a headlamp, put on the reflective jacket and head out into the night with my pooch (who has his own reflective jacket).

We pull hard on the edge of the evening, refusing to submit. We run. Or ski. Sometimes in the streets. Sometimes in the woods. Sometimes in solitude.

A moon can soften the landscape, etch out the mountains and trees in friendly companionship. In the night, everything feels faster, especially on skis. The snow—it catches you, softens the blow, when you fall. Flying down a hill with only the small fan of light illuminating the immediate trail, every upcoming turn and obstacle hides in the shadows. It is a bit like life—how the future hangs so close, so unknown.

It's good practice: to move forward this way with faith, a small snowplow of caution, a squeal of delight.

Sometimes I go with a friend, turn a quiet Tuesday night into a private revel. Two beams of light in the pines, shrieks of laughter (maybe fear) on the descents, a trio of dogs fanning out into the trees to track the deer.

And sometimes, I go where the crowds are. For all the winter hibernation that takes places in these mountains, folks have a remarkable ability to rise to the occasion and rile it up. As though their heartbeats depend on it, they gather. Last week, it was the tradition of the Full Moon Ski Party. Kegs, bonfires, music. Silhouettes of anonymous skiers striding through the night.

I learned a while back that if I met the physical pain halfway, if I gave it some of my own energy, it didn't seem so unbearable. I think the winter might be like this, too. Meet it out there. You might find some beauty in the darkness.

This essay first appeared on the author's blog "The Nervous Breakdown."

Part II
The People

MUSIC OF THE MOUNTAINS

By Dan Berggren

What shall we sing, while the fire burns down?
We can sing only specifics, time's rambling tune,
the places we have seen, the faces we have known.
—*Annie Dillard, "The Galapagos" from* Life on the Rocks

Hello, I'm Harry Wilson's grandson—Dorothy's boy."
That's how I introduced myself at Cecil Butler's front door, the winter of 1975. With a voice as deep as a well, he invited me into the farmhouse where he'd been born eighty-nine years before, into the kitchen where the wood stove crackled and the refrigerator hummed and into his world of mountain music.

"Harry's grandson, eh? Come on in. Oh, you got a guitar. Ruth, I wished you'd bring my fiddle out…would ya honey?"

Cecil introduced me to his second wife, calling her his "spring chicken" since she was only seventy. Together they made me feel right at home, and the search for more stories about my grandfather began.

Thanks to my mother, keeper of the family history, I learned I was the fifth generation to live on the family farm just over the mountain from the Butler place. The Wilsons, like so many others who settled in the Adirondack wilderness, came from Ireland during the potato famines of the mid-1800s; they brought their families, their customs and their music. My mother described a typical summer evening during her childhood: "We used to pick berries all day and then hull berries all evening by the light of the kerosene lamp in the dark kitchen. Little tin pans on our laps and [Aunt] Eloise singing to us helped to pass the time."

Once when Grandpa had pneumonia, a cousin came to do the cooking and help take care of my mother and her brother. "He used to sing for us in the evening," my mother told me. "And Van and I would learn all these old songs. He used to bake big pancakes in the morning and sing to us at night."

Fortunately, I too grew up in a singing family that was tuned in to the sights and sounds of the wilderness that surrounded the farm. Uncle Van took me hunting and taught me how to become part of the woods, to blend in and listen. My mother knew that those loud "shots" I heard on a twenty-five-below-zero night were not hunters jacking deer but sap freezing in the pines. Mountain music is organic. It grows out of the wild, the civilized and the borders between them.

> *Be still. Be as quiet as a forest at midnight.*
> *So still that when the temperature drops,*
> *Freezing the sap in the white pines,*
> *You hear it snap. Be still.*
> "Be Still," ©1999 Dan Berggren

Two years before my knock on Cecil's door, I was stationed overseas and feeling homesick. This prompted a song about Grandpa, who seemed to be at one with the land.

> *Harry helped his father run the farm*
> *And kept his own family fed and warm.*
> *He looked at the mountains and he knew he was free.*
> *Oh, how I wish that were me.*
> *He always did the best that he could.*
> *He never forgot: the earth was good.*
> "Harry," ©1973 Dan Berggren

After morning chores, Harry had a mail route, one of the first Rural Free Delivery routes in the Adirondacks. He'd go to the post office at the Four Corners in Olmstedville, help sort the mail, put it in his leather pouch and head to Irishtown, Loch Muller and Hoffman and then home to Leonardsville.

Wanting to learn more about my ancestors, my neighborhood and its rich history, I traveled the mail route carrying the old pouch. It ended up in Cecil's lap on that first visit.

"That's good leather," he said. "Harry used to carry it with horses, you know, good while ago. I know darn well I seen him put his hand in there and take out mail and hand it to me."

I also brought along a tape recorder to capture some of the memories. The combination of the mail pouch and Cecil's fiddle triggered many stories, songs and dance calls from the past. "I've played for square dances for sixty-six years," he told me. "Kitchen dances, like this here, you know."

After he'd tuned up his fiddle, Ruth cautioned him, "Don't tire yourself all out."

"No, that won't tire me any. Music always pepped me up, you know."

Then he launched into a dance tune, a reel he learned over in Irishtown from Walter O'Connor. "It's the Irishtown Breakdown. Oh, it's a good piece, and boy, you can shake your feet on it too, when you get on the corners. You know, if my hands was right, and my fingers was right, I could run in a lot of variations on that."

Although Cecil learned to fiddle by ear, both he and his sister were taught to sing their scales by a mother who played organ and violin. Everyone in the family sang; that was simply a part of life in the mountains.

"When I was about maybe eleven years old, I couldn't play a lot of pieces but I played some pretty good you know, they'd dance to it," Cecil said. In addition to playing and calling for dances, he made pack baskets and fishing creels, produced maple syrup, did some carpentry, worked in a logging camp and was a hunting and fishing guide and a trapper. Like many in the North Woods, he learned to survive by embracing the vast wilderness that surrounded his small piece of civilization. He grew up in a time when neighbors traded work, when a kitchen could hold four couples for a square dance, when birthdays and holidays were celebrated with family stories and a hymn-sing around the pump organ and when the mailman not only carried letters and packages but also shared news of the neighborhood: "When our daughter Phyllis was born, we held her up to the window so's Harry could see and he'd tell others on the route that the Butlers had their baby."

Ten years after meeting Cecil, I released an Adirondack music album that included some of his comments and fiddling. Imagine my surprise upon receiving a letter from Phyllis saying how wonderful it was to "hear Dad's voice again" on the recording. Imagine the honor of being asked to sing at Phyllis's ninetieth birthday party, just outside the window where she witnessed the world for the first time and gave Harry some good news to share. Imagine the great delight of playing the tune Cecil had taught me for his great-granddaughter Amy's wedding, held in the ancient apple orchard of that same homestead.

Our kitchen session on that distant winter's day created a bond across generations and continues to fuel a passion for honest, authentic music. These are not words and notes longing for the past. It is music that creates a new sense of community each time it comes alive in song or dance. It is music that holds both the beauty and the harshness of life, all of its hopes and fears and embodies an unspoken understanding that we are a part of the interdependent web of nature. It is music as fresh and vital and fragile as the seedling that sprouts from the cone of an old white pine when it finds fertile soil.

In the summer of 1981, a few months before he died, Cecil and I had our last visit. We sang and laughed; he told some of the same stories, plus a few new ones, and I listened. We shook hands and said goodbye. As I turned to leave, he gave his North Country benediction: "I wouldn't mind if you lived next door."

FULL CIRCLE:
THE JOURNEY OF ONE ARTIST

By Tim Fortune

Memories have a way of simplifying our past experiences. Reaching back and extracting these moments in time, based on our selective memories, provides a glimpse into the shaping of our identity. Because we are the sum of all past experiences, it follows that an artist's sensibilities and artistic expressions are shaped by the connections with people and community.

Growing up in Saranac Lake left an imprint on me that has never faded. In many ways, it was like a Norman Rockwell painting: riding my tricycle to Marty's Grocery Store, buying a creamsicle, pedaling across the street to swim at the Lake Flower Beach, full of trees, long since removed to add two extra lanes for traffic. At one point in my life, I realized I could live and die in the same two-block radius. There was my grade school, grocery store, doctor's office, beach and, finally, a funeral home, my family's business. Luckily, though, I did venture beyond those two blocks.

There are a great number of advantages to growing up in a small community such as Saranac Lake: extended networks of friends and family, safety, walks to services, a clean environment and many more. The disadvantages become apparent upon leaving one's safe, insulated setting: exposure to diverse ethnicities; broad cultural offerings; and, in my case, art and art-making.

I was quite content to play sports but only dabbled in art as a kind of diversion from the "real" subjects being taught. The nuns at Pius X Central High School were good educators and stern taskmasters, for which I am now grateful.

After marrying my high school sweetheart, Diana Mason, in 1972, we moved to Florida for sixteen years while also periodically living in Philadelphia, New York City, Rome and Venice, Italy. These separations from home gave me a fresh perspective on my relationship with the landscape of the Adirondacks. I realized that we had grown up in the middle of a unique park, larger than several of our largest national parks combined.

On our return visits to Saranac Lake, there was always an internal sigh of relief, followed by a deep breath, as we turned off Interstate 87 at Exit 30 heading toward Keene Valley and the mountains. Gaining altitude, ears popping, blood pressure lowering—we were home.

In 1988, Diana and I, with our three cats, moved back to Saranac Lake and started fixing up an old family farmhouse and barn on thirty-five acres in the nearby hamlet of Bloomingdale. If you've ever watched reruns of *The Andy Griffith Show* on TV, then you have an idea of the town's similarity to the fictitious town of Mayberry.

Our house, barn and broken-down chicken coop are on a bog next to a meandering brook. Cold Brook is not only beautiful with its beaver dams, ducks and herons; it is also, I am convinced, the birthplace of all the nasty, voracious black flies in the Adirondacks.

Living next to the brook and being able to walk the property to witness the changes nature imparts helped foster a more intimate connection with the landscape. The sounds of the wind, birds and animals give added depth to my work. Photographs cannot convey what the senses witness in the outdoors.

My oils and watercolors are more than a visual record. They should, if my intentions work, produce an aesthetic experience beyond what the experience superficially represents. Is there a sense of mystery? Does the painting raise questions that encourage discussion, and, most important to me, does it create a consistent personal vision of my relationship with nature?

My dedication to what I paint has varied, but a constant over the years has been water. I have always been drawn to the sound, movement, changing forms, reflection and transparency of water. The lakes, streams and waterfalls of the Adirondacks, the Intracoastal Waterway and ocean of Florida, the two summers in Venice—how could I not paint water? It's visible, colorful, smooth, rough, abstract in its effect on images and always a great source of interest. Its visual elements are ever-changing; it is a challenge to convey their dynamic qualities in a static state.

My paintings are built largely on instincts, on gut feelings, directing my choice of medium, scale and effect. This is important because if it is true to your essence as an artist and a person, then it will more likely have an intangible, universal effect on viewers. This cannot be easily explained but could be referred to as the mystery of the piece.

The relatively isolated, low population base of the North Country relates directly to how art is created. This usually involves a solitary experience in the studio or in front of a computer screen or playing an instrument or experiencing nature. Alone with our thoughts yet actively engaged, allowing ideas to free-flow, for me is much easier in nature. Creation of a painting is a collaboration of images, ideas and art materials guided by the courage to challenge myself. Thrown into this mix are the dramatic changes of the seasons, which force me into different modes of thought and feeling.

Winter is my most productive time. Nature is resting under a cold blanket of snow, and I am in my studio/gallery in Saranac Lake exploring new approaches or expanding on already established ones. If I can't wait to get to the studio to work on a painting, then I know I'm on the right track. My most recent self-imposed challenge is painting watercolors on a large scale of four by six feet.

Spring brings renewed energy just in the nick of time. New growth and new marketing plans, new ways to survive in the Adirondacks. It takes creativity to survive and thrive in the Adirondacks, and those who manage to make a livelihood are deeply rewarded, usually in non-monetary ways. As I've often said, I didn't move back to the North Country to get rich, and so far my plan is working.

When summer finally arrives, my large watercolors are complete and I begin producing small oils and watercolors in preparation for an influx of visitors to our town. The rhythms of the North Country keep one challenged and engaged in life, and since change is vital to artists, then in what better environment to create?

The commute to my working studio/galleries is never boring; it changes constantly. The seven-mile trip from Bloomingdale to Saranac Lake begins with a view of Whiteface Mountain. Two country antique shops are followed by a pasture of grazing cattle that we watch grow over the year. There are also llamas and the occasional deer, and wild turkeys visit a potato farm. The owners of this farm feed extra potatoes to the very pleased cattle across the street. The last two miles or so, the beautiful Saranac River meanders next to the road, the most naturally appealing part of the journey. Except for a misplaced school bus garage, this commute is luckily my favorite drive in the Adirondacks and quite an inspiration on my way to the studio.

I named my studio/gallery the Small Fortune Studio because it is quite small, not because my works cost a small fortune. It has functioned quite well since I opened in 1994. One of the joys of having a business in downtown Saranac Lake is knowing that I am adding to the vitality and diversity of the town.

In participating in the cultural present, my business will be part of the history of the downtown area. To see Saranac Lake evolve into a growing arts community has been a wonderful thing to witness and participate in. Artists need only a location that supports their approach to art-making and other artists and art-lovers, which Saranac Lake now provides. It's a more diverse community than before, of people who seem to be closer than in other towns. Maybe this closeness is encouraged by the long, frigid winters that prompt the need to be close both physically and emotionally.

There is a deep relationship with friends, family and others here. One direct result was an art project opportunity that helped me express these feelings. I applied for a grant from the New York State Council on the Arts facilitated through the Arts Council of the Northern Adirondacks. The grant's primary criterion was to directly engage members of the community in an artistic endeavor. I won the grant with the concept of creating a large self-portrait (approximately three feet by five feet) using one-inch square photographs donated by anyone from the village who wanted to participate. I titled the piece "It Takes A Village To Raise An Artist."

I created a large wood surface on which I drew a one-inch grid. I placed this background form in the Blue Moon Café with a donation box next to it for photographs. People donated not only photos of themselves and family members but also of their pets, which I, of course, included. The most touching were the photographs of deceased loved ones, both people and pets, which broadened the scope of the mosaic to a memorial and moved me deeply.

I superimposed the grid over a photograph of my face. As I placed the one-inch squares of people's faces extracted from the donated photos, my own image emerged gradually over the course of four months, as witnessed daily by customers and visitors at the café.

I am still getting questions about the piece. Its final resting place is in the permanent collection of the Adirondack Museum in Blue Mountain Lake, where it will be protected for years to come as a testament to how much of an impact communities can have on our lives.

Just as this grant opportunity generated the idea for the mosaic, I believe everything happens for a reason and we must always be receptive to various opportunities that may go unnoticed. Schopenhauer, the noted philosopher, states, "just as dreams are imposed by an unconscious awareness, so too your life is composed by the will within you. And just as people whom you have met apparently by chance become leading agents in the structure of your life, so too you will give meaning to the lives of others. The whole thing is like a symphony, everything unconsciously structuring everything else, moved by the one will to life, which is the universal will in nature."

As these ever-present events shape our lives, our distant past continues to influence our choices as well. People are drawn to Saranac Lake for its healthy approach to life. Friends and family are extremely important in the North Country. We tend to be sensitive to each other's needs and willing to reach out and contribute to the well being of our community. Our historic connection to the days when Saranac Lake was a famous tuberculosis cure center speaks to us from the past, encouraging those who have an open heart to care about our neighbors and to depend on them when in need. The Adirondack Medical Center, the abundance of doctors and the healing arts businesses in the area are a direct result of our shared history. The mind-body connection is no longer a New Age theory but a proven benefit to recovering patients. The healing arts in Saranac Lake are thriving, with yoga, massage and related complementary approaches to improving the quality of life—another example of the effect history has on us all.

The visual arts were also an important aspect of our history and connected to the curative power of the Adirondacks. An artists' guild was created years ago as a way of letting the patients produce works through their own efforts, thus lifting their spirits. This healing approach to living continues to help form my character as a person and artist.

I derive great pleasure in helping other artists however I am able. In 1998, I started the Adirondack Artists Guild, a cooperative gallery that has grown to fourteen artists. To see their camaraderie and the effect they are having on our community through their exhibitions and special events gives me great pride.

Since 1994, the Small Fortune Studio has continued the history of the presence of a Fortune merchant in downtown Saranac Lake. There have been Fortune clothing stores, butchers, furniture and casket sales and a funeral home going back five generations. To have this connection to the history of Saranac Lake gives me an eerie sense that my life seemed to lead me to this point.

Our histories have a way of sneaking up on us and tapping us on the shoulder, saying, "See, that's why you are the way you are, so embrace it and keep an open heart." As the poet T.S. Eliot said, "The end of all our exploring will be to arrive where we started and know the place for the first time."

THE TAO OF WOODPILES

By Phil Sallos

I am lingering in bed this morning with neither woman nor dog beside me, but I can hear them moving beyond my sight. The walls of the old house are thin and uninsulated, and they admit sounds with the same impartiality they allow ghosts and mice.

Marion is in the woodshed splitting kindling for the morning fire. From two rooms and a hall and a flight of stairs away, through three closed doors, I can hear every nuance of her work, can hear her ax striking the upright bolts, can hear the sound of the parted pieces bouncing against the block and landing on the earthen floor, over and over again.

I am not really a lazy man. I have helped Marion many a long day splitting heating wood for the big stove downstairs, tackling with wedges and maul the great gnarly rounds that Dennis Muzzy's brother dumped in her backyard for two hundred bucks after she'd asked him for straight-grained, medium-sized stock. He probably got a good laugh leaving this gentle, soft-spoken woman with a mountain of butt-ends and crotches. And she living alone there in that leaky old house—she'd probably have to hire a team of teenage boys or a man with a splitting machine just to break the stuff down to a size she could carry.

He was almost completely wrong. If he laughed, his laughter went nowhere but back into his own face. I helped when I had free days. I even borrowed a friend's hydraulic splitter one afternoon and nearly wrecked it. Mainly, Marion made the mountain smaller, steadily taking it down during the short autumn hours she had between coming home from her job and dinnertime or fitting it between other chores on weekends and constantly criticizing herself for not doing enough.

The mountain is gone now. I helped Marion because I wanted to. She really didn't need it. There are still a few nasty chunks scattered about like boulders left behind by a glacier. When she's in the mood, Marion tackles one even though she's got a new mountain in her yard brought to her by a man in Malone. She paid a lot more, but she got what she wanted this time; now she's in the woodshed splitting kindling, and I am still upstairs drowsy under the covers.

I love to lie here listening to Marion work on wood. Splitting wood is no big deal, you know. Anyone can do it, but everyone does it differently. I know a woman who takes great pride in her husband's axemanship. She told me once, "I don't know anybody who can split wood like Marion except Cootch, and he's the best I've seen. They're fast enough; but the thing is, they're so smooth. It looks like no effort's made at all, and they can go on that way for hours. Next thing you know, there's enough split to keep your stove filled for a week."

So through the walls and doors and floors I listen to Marion working, splitting wood the way she plays her banjo or the way she sings—the way she aspires to live her life: smoothly, harmoniously, consistently, competently, without flash and flourish but in a way that unmistakably makes music.

The thwack of the ax and the thump on the floor have stopped. I hear footfalls between the garden and the house and the jingling of Ginger's collar, the heavy door opening, boots and dog nails in the hall turning the corner into the kitchen, the clatter of an armful of maple hitting the floorboards beside the stove.

Marion making a fire. Marion making a fire to warm herself and her dog and her not really lazy friend still upstairs. My being here doesn't matter. I know she would be doing these things whether I was in her house or not. This is part of the rhythm of her morning, like a moving meditation that quietly nourishes her spirit.

I have always admired Marion's strength, her stamina, her self-sufficiency. I had seen those qualities in her from the beginning, but I don't believe I ever questioned where they came from or what they required, and I began to accept them so much as innate parts of her—as though they were things born into, not worked for—that I slowly lost track of their importance to her.

Strength, stamina and self-sufficiency—but most of all self-sufficiency. Maybe just now, as I hear the wood being arranged in the firebox, maybe just now I am beginning to understand the meaning of Marion's self-sufficiency:

that inside this understated woman there is an unstated need to engage life unassisted and on her own terms and which is inseparable from her own sense of who she is and who she can be. And under these covers by myself, as I hear Marion moving in other rooms on this mist-shrouded morning, I think I am beginning to understand also that her strength and stamina and self-sufficiency require a rhythmic reaffirmation of her own place in her own life that the unlimited presence of others will eventually, inevitably disrupt.

The mountain of difficult wood is gone. I helped Marion with it because I wanted to. She really didn't need it, and as the house warms now from the split pieces of a new pile, I wonder if perhaps she'd have needed me more not to help. Sometimes I believe that I can see something of the Tao of life and its woodpiles, that there are times when the intimacy of sharing can become an interference and the comfort of companionship a cramp—that there are times when a woman must stand by herself beside a roaring stove, look out into an empty winter yard and whisper within her heart, "I can. I did. I am."

IN THE SHADOW OF THE WALLS

By Lita Kelly

I wasn't afraid of the walls—just of what was behind them. I was young; they were old. I was small; they were tall—and long and deep and impenetrable. On sunny days, their warm glow was almost appealing. On cloudy days, they were forbidding and very sad. On rainy days, I felt a penetrating chill as I quickly glanced at them and then looked away. At those times, I felt enveloped by gray and darkness; though the walls never really surrounded me, they surrounded my senses. The odor of their hot, moist post-thunderstorm concrete blended perfectly with the fragrance of damp, warm oil wafting from the wet asphalt of the street. I often found myself stopping to listen to the echoes of passing vehicles bouncing off the walls as they would off a mountain. After a blizzard, I admired their silver coats of snow and ice. I wore a coat, too, but it couldn't keep out the chill that was part of growing up in the shadow of the walls of Clinton Prison in Dannemora, New York.

Those walls told tales to anyone who knew how to listen. Some were melodramas, some tragedies. To post–World War II families, they told tales of men like my dad who were fathers with new full-time jobs, food on the table and a car in the driveway. To the wives of prison guards, they whispered that those guarding the prison from its shoulders were also community "babysitters" they could count on to know what was going on in the village. We all felt safe because they were there. From the stories my father told, I couldn't help feeling that the stories the walls told the prisoners had to be of isolation, loneliness, intimidation and fear.

From the time I went to kindergarten, with the memory of a five-year-old, my tales were much different. Those walls, after all, were my next-door neighbors. I lived only one gas station (my personal candy store) and one house away from the southeast guard tower. My stories were more like fairy tales, the stuff of dreams—and nightmares—woven into a tapestry that had begun to be fashioned over a century earlier.

Dannemora was born over a hundred years before I was. In 1842, Ransom Cook was given the job of locating a prison that could keep its convicts actively—and profitably—employed. His search was rewarded with the discovery of an iron ore mine at the Averill Ore Bed in what would soon become Dannemora, a name borrowed from a small iron mining town in Sweden. Upon Cook's recommendation, the state of New York bought two hundred acres of land and its mining concerns from Charles Averill and F.L.C. Sailly. On June 3, 1845, the first fifty convicts arrived wearing striped uniforms and balls and chains. They'd blazed a trail through Cadyville forest land and began to build their own twenty-foot cedar prison walls. Soon after, to a place cold enough in winter to be named "Little Siberia," came the new villagers—a few merchants and men taking jobs as guards who brought their wives and children with them.

There were always children in Dannemora—children growing up in a village founded on crime, children living a day-to-day existence that was far from average, yet very normal…to them. As children do, they had to adapt to their surroundings, just as I did many years later.

Children who lived in Dannemora's prison town were like children anywhere. They needed love, guidance, food and clothing. They played games and make-believe, went to school and to church on Sunday, fought together over childish disputes and laughed together over shared secrets and private jokes. Of course. But there was always a difference, to the child of Ransom Cook's day or to a child like me, growing up in the aftermath of World War II.

Our fathers, who fought in the war and came home to a world changed in their minds forever, weren't like other fathers, who worked in industry, sales, farming, the medical field or teaching. Our fathers had to know how to fight, to shoot, to second-guess some master manipulators and how to keep quiet about it all at home, skills they'd learned as soldiers and had hoped to leave behind. Still, few of them refused the opportunity to work "behind the walls." Like my dad, many men left college or good jobs to serve their country, only to come home from the war to find that the best opportunity for "unskilled employment" was a job behind the walls of Clinton Prison.

Jobs were waiting, as was a very new way of life. My father knew he was lucky to have a state job, so one day in August my family, including this wide-eyed three-year-old, rolled into Dannemora and stayed.

Dad may have been considered unskilled then, but he wasn't for long. The education he quickly received behind the walls became my textbook—one that took me decades to begin to understand. On its cover was my own mental portrait of the gates of Dannemora, the only opening in the walls that a child could peek through to try to figure out where her Daddy went when he was let in by the "keeper of the gate," to stride quickly out of my sight.

As time went on, the simplicity of life in a prison town lent consistency to our families, support for each church's parishioners and pride in our schools, which was of prime importance. I spent my summers riding to the Chazy Lake beach on a bus filled with singing kids. I learned more than how to swim on those lazy afternoons. I learned to love watching the days move by as if they had given up the race, deciding to let the tortoise take home the prize. Parents thought nothing of telling us to go play outdoors and not return home until dinnertime. We found every shortcut imaginable to make it to the playground as fast as possible. There were board games to play, jungle gym apparatus and swings to play on, softball and baseball games to play or cheer for and bubblegum contests. Everyone knew each other. We played together or wandered fearlessly alone. My brothers and sisters and I donned costumes and went trick-or-treating together, hitting nearly every house in town. Not realizing that I was growing older, too, I watched older kids and wondered if I'd ever be that pretty/smart/old. I dreamed of someday making my friends and neighbors proud of me, the third of six children, searching for an identity with a budding singing voice that occasionally earned me a smidgen of praise or a rewarding smile.

I enjoyed living in a town that, most of the time, I "just knew" was perfectly safe. As children, we didn't know the meaning of danger. In truth, we weren't always safe, but no one wanted to admit it in public, especially the grown-ups. As an old friend recently told me, growing up in Dannemora was wonderful for her. She seldom took note of the prison. It was just something that was there, except…except the time her father came home from work with a torn shirt and had to sit the family down to explain that he'd been in a scuffle, but that it was nothing…really. Her story triggered one of my own—one that brought me the first chill of fear for my father's life.

I'll never forget that day. Dad came home from the prison, obviously upset. He'd just made it through a potential prison break that, thankfully, fizzled in its tracks—dying before it could turn into a nightmare. The break had been carefully planned. It was simple: as the convicts were released to go to the recreation yard, the guard on duty would be overpowered and killed when access to the outside was at hand.

That guard would have been Dad. He'd agreed to work for another guard that day. I could picture it all unfolding: Dad quickly covering the ground between the gate and the cellblock, hearing iron gates closing behind him with a large key turning in each lock to make each long corridor secure and then taking his place outside two long rows of cells. As he later told the story to my mother, a convict he'd made a point to treat fairly when a little kindness could make the man feel more worthy of respect called Dad over to his cell. After expressing surprise that Dad was on duty that day, he informed my father of the imminent prison break. He wasn't going to let my father be killed. He didn't. My dad was able to leave the prison after his shift, shaken but physically unharmed. That convict had his pride. I still had my dad. I still give thanks to that man over and over. I always will.

It wasn't at all unusual to be playing outdoors and glance up to see a group of convicts coming toward me, walking down the middle of the street, on their way to a job detail. They weren't allowed near the sidewalk, which was our boundary. We were to move back toward the house, staying well behind those sidewalks. Smiling and waving was forbidden, which seemed sad because most of the men didn't look much different from the men I knew. Many of the prisoners weren't white, which I noticed but never thought to question. We didn't talk about it at home; it was just fact. The only black people I saw at the time were related to the convicts. When buses pulled in from out of town and people began to file out and go inside the prison, we noticed. There were so many, and they were so sad. The fact that they looked different from the people I saw every day took a back seat to the looks on their faces. Knowing they'd come for a visit, only to have to turn away and leave their loved ones alone again, made me sad, too.

The first black person I met was a little girl about my age. She was walking east on the sidewalk opposite the front wall. I was walking west. We started to talk. Her dad was in prison, and she was going to see that day. I couldn't imagine not seeing my dad every day. My dad was in the prison that day, too, but he'd be coming home that night when the wall opened and let him go.

I asked the little girl with the lovely black braids and big smile what her name was. She told me it was Lita, just like mine. We both smiled and laughed, enjoying a great moment. Neither of us had known any other Litas, but now that had changed. We truly had something in common.

I often dreamed about meeting her again, but that dream never materialized. Once in a while, she'd come to mind, and I'd wonder if she'd forgotten me. I remember wishing that her father could have gone home with her that day, a dream she must have shared. I never knew her father, and she never knew mine. Would she have understood why this big, kindhearted Irishman was one of her father's jailers, someone her dad may even have feared? Those are questions with lives of their own that may never be answered.

Lita left the walls of Clinton Prison behind her that day. I didn't. I stayed. Dannemora was my home.

Days in Dannemora bring visions of life filled with friends, activities and creative ways to spend our time. In the light of day, we children had nothing to lose. With some very specific boundaries to protect us, we engaged in many pursuits, some useful and some not. There were potholders to make and sell to earn money for the fair, michigans to deliver for a woman who was an admirable entrepreneur, visits to the local bar and grill for great burgers and homemade cherry Cokes, biking to the store or post office, frog-jumping tournaments on a neighbor's front porch. Those were the days.

Then there were the nights. For me, they were different.

When the sun went down on Dannemora, I had to face my fear. I can't put a finger on a time when things changed for me. Over time, I became more wary and reserved when it came to the prisoners who shared my village. We were separated by Cook Street, but I finally realized Cook Street wasn't very wide.

My sisters and I shared a bedroom that faced north, overlooking a portion of the prison wall shielding the prison's shop from the rest of the world. The presence of the shop was unnerving to all the inmates of that bedroom. One of my sisters was afraid of the orange-tinged shop lights with their eerie flickering. At night, she would wake up, fearing that the shops were on fire. She'd wonder how hot the walls would have to be before they collapsed and try to calculate whether or not their height would cause them to land on our house.

From my child's perspective, I became certain that anyone behind those shop windows could see into our room. I took immediate action. I began to shut the window blinds at dusk every night. If only I'd realized that if I couldn't see through their windows, they couldn't see through mine…

Though I shut out every possible visual contact with the prison each night, I began to feel that I needed to know everything about any way I might have potential contact with men from behind that wall. I found myself hanging on every word of every story of any potential escape that came my way. Since Dad wouldn't tell us kids anything, I overheard his tales when I was supposed to be asleep upstairs and my parents were having coffee in the dining room below. I overheard a few good ones—but personally experienced a couple more.

Stories of escape attempts from Clinton Prison are numerous and tantalizing. Not every escape failed, though the majority did. One of my dad's best stories was of a very short inmate from the State Hospital for the Criminally Insane, a building due east of the main prison. Allegedly, this convict got away from the hospital around Halloween and walked through the village with a bag over his head. He was mistaken for a child pretending to be in costume. Instead of candy, though, he was in search of something very different, something he couldn't have.

His freedom was short-lived. He was discovered at Sweeney's gas station by some high school students with guns. The convict had taken shelter under a truck. His effort to pull himself up into the chassis was unsuccessful; the students noticed one of the man's legs sticking out and quickly took care of the situation with an authority their fathers must have appreciated. I heard that tale many times after I became an adult—whenever Dad was in the mood for a prison story. It was one of my favorites.

Dad didn't need to tell me about the escape attempt that occurred on July 23, 1960. I was there.

Remembering an earlier escape attempt that resulted in the destruction of my mom's flower and asparagus gardens by many officers' boots as they ran through what could have been labeled a "chase scene," I listened intently to a telephone conversation between my grandmother and my dad as he informed her that some prisoners from the State Hospital had escaped and two of them were headed toward her camp in Chazy Lake. My sister and I were there to spend the night, so we locked the doors, went on "alert" and stayed close together. Many phone calls later, we learned from Dad that one of the men had been arrested trying to hitch a ride from a state trooper. We stayed on guard. It rained that night so we really didn't miss going outside.

The next morning we walked behind the camp and found boot prints in the mud just below our bedroom window. Once the police were notified, there was an intensive search of the area. The "con" was found a few camps east of ours, where he'd taken shelter for the night. That night he was back where he belonged, and we were back enjoying the stars and s'mores around the campfire, mindful of loving warnings that began to be a regular part of daily life.

Harvesting what he'd learned from experiences behind the walls, Dad began to teach us crucial life skills. We Kelly kids began to learn how to survive. Relative innocence was over. His girls learned how to defend themselves with a few solid moves inspired by the marines. Checking the backseat of a car before entering became a habit. Life had changed. We were all growing up. Our futures began to take root and grow. It was time to prepare.

Dad and Mom were determined to offer each of us the possibility of advanced education, giving us opportunities that World War II had denied my father. Looking ahead at college costs and other educational opportunities, we knew a move was imminent. It soon became reality.

Driving away from the village my dad loved, we moved into a home almost next door to Plattsburgh State University. I walked to high school and walked to college. Over time, marriage, children and careers triggered growth in our family. I may have grown older, but I never really grew away from my years in a prison town—*my* prison town.

Every time I drove through Dannemora to go to camp, I listened to the whispering of my memories. Whenever life outside the confines and contentments of Dannemora became out of balance, I'd return—physically or in my dreams. During the nights, my dream world often took me back to the home on Clark Street, the playground I used to love or the stream where my sisters and I waited for the resident hermit to find us and perhaps say, "Hello." Eventually, I found myself driving to Dannemora rather than through it, driving through streets I used to walk, looking at houses that were not as huge as they once seemed to be, people who were not as tall, streets that were not as long.

Dannemora has changed, as has my perception of it. My childhood nest looks different now—older and altered by time. Most of the businesses I knew have been closed and shuttered. I applaud the new ones that came to take their places, while wishing there were more there for the villagers of today. St. Joseph's Catholic School is gone, as is Dannemora High School, where I studied, twirled baton, sang in the chorus and played my first instrument. Buses travel the streets now, picking up the children and taking them off the mountain to Saranac Central, taking them away.

The village sounds different, too. The playground is often empty now, yet it will always be alive in my memory. I treasure an image of me finally succeeding in climbing to the top of the jungle gym. The occasional bounce of a basketball tossed toward a rusty hoop by a couple of high school boys breaks a silence that now seems foreign. The sounds of laughter and the tears that filled Dannemora's streets in the 1950s and '60s are muted now as children stay indoors, perhaps playing video games and working with their computers. So solitary; so different.

Only life behind the walls has remained relatively the same. The guards still report for their shifts, sporting neatly pressed uniforms and a necessary suit of emotional armor—modern-day soldiers offering protection and salvation to those they love and serve. Office personnel, cooks, teachers and nurses still walk through the gates, bringing life to the prison and its inmates in often unexpected ways. The Church of the Good Thief rests behind those old prison walls, offering the prisoners a life of faith in a world of conflict.

What do I believe in now, years after I first walked through the doors of 31 Clark Street? I believe that the modern world still has room for the vibrancy that can be found in Dannemora's human legacy. Our parents' lives are eternally linked with our own, though they may no longer walk beside us. Despite the passing of time, their values still pervade the streets of my little town, riding on the shoulders of their children, grandchildren and great-grandchildren. New people and new ideas are melding with the minds of those who have always lived and loved within Dannemora's walls—not behind those old concrete barriers that shadowed my childhood, but within the walls of houses, apartments, town buildings and stores and within the walls of all of our hearts. Those are the real walls of Dannemora.

MOVING FORWARD

By Margaret Olsen

When I first came to the Adirondacks for college four years ago, I was, truth be told, underwhelmed. Having grown up and lived my entire life in Seattle, I was used to nature in my face, was accustomed to the spires of mountains like Rainier and Baker looming over the cityscape, though they are both many miles away. I was used to large bodies of water, both fresh and saline, and familiarized by the perpetual green of Douglas firs all year-round. Maybe because of this, I was also more inclined to see myself outside of the natural landscape, more apt to interpret nature as disconnected from the day-to-day business of human activity. Nature was something I went *out* to experience. Despite its eco-friendly persona, Seattle is a metropolis, and as temperate rain systems sweep inland from the Pacific Ocean and over the Olympic Mountains, they are drawn above the city to the North Cascades, where they dump their predictably wet and heavy loads. In winter or summer, weather doesn't fluctuate a great deal, and "nature" keeps to itself outside city limits, despite a subtly pervasive influence: one may notice the green-washed side-panel advertisements on the metro buses, championing what is, ironically, a generally shoddy municipal public transit system.

In the Adirondack North Country of upstate New York, however, I was to find an entirely different experience. The vistas of world-class mountain ranges dropping dramatically from the clouds into the endless Pacific morphed into (barely) rolling farmland hills and valleys. Although St. Lawrence University proclaims itself to be "nestled in the foothills of the Adirondacks," this is a bit of a reach. The land that unfolds on all sides from campus stretches out unbroken like the blanket on a just-made hospital bed, uniform and devoid of many noteworthy natural features: a couple of slow-moving rivers, a few wooded thickets, cornfields and grazing pasture. It's roughly a half-hour drive from my campus to the Adirondack Park, nearly thirty miles before anything remotely mountainous.

I found the late summer and early autumn nice enough, when everything was soft and green, trees were full and then, suddenly, tinged with early indications of changing time—the adolescent yellows and orange sherbets that would soon bleed to red and drift downward with the onset of wind, rain and then snow. The color was, indeed, beautiful, but it seemed to pass in the blink of an eye—I couldn't orient myself to the brevity of seasonal shifts, and the inevitable monotony that followed. It was a shock to the system, vegetation falling from the trees, everything dying and decaying underfoot, leaving only the brittle bones of branches in a gray sky to remind me that life was shutting down, turning off, until spring. It wasn't beautiful to me and became just tolerable when the snow fell, freezing and covering the slop of rotted leaves and mud holes. And that was the first time I understood the concept of hibernation the way an animal might, understood the risk of being outside after dark with no gloves—perhaps the first time I experienced my own frailty on a regular basis.

And so it was slowly, over time, that I learned to realign my perspectives on nature. Every autumn I spend in the North Country I feel the initial sensations of hopelessness creeping up on me, trying to convince me that this will be the longest, hardest winter yet, that I will lose all sense of motivation and spend the winter months working just enough to get by in my classes, drinking too much and ignoring the future. The feelings come more slowly now, whenever the average daily temperature drops another degree or two, and just as slowly, I remind myself not to give in to them.

When I started college, I knew nothing about the Adirondacks—I chose St. Lawrence because it seemed to epitomize what I thought I wanted from my college education: the liberal arts and a cozy East Coast setting, with a solid reputation to boot. I didn't know where to hike or paddle, where or how to find edible fungus, the best winter climbs or the best place to grab a bite in Tupper Lake. I didn't know about the seasonal farmer's market just down the street from campus, where you can buy everything from local maple syrup to local wines, cheeses and produce. I couldn't appreciate how the landscape tied into the local economy and knew nothing of the environmental campaigns that fight everyday to protect the largest wilderness area in the lower forty-eight states. I didn't know that Ralph

Waldo Emerson and Theodore Roosevelt once wandered and mused in these mountains, inspiring the works that would evolve mainstream attitudes toward nature and later serve as foundations for the entire philosophy of environmentalism. In other words, I didn't have much of a reason to love this particular environment. Certainly, some of these things I might have learned anywhere, but most of them are the collected byproducts of having learned about, and how to care for, a place I inhabit.

The Adirondacks are more significant to the broader environmental and climate discussion today than perhaps ever before. The Adirondack wilderness has seen more rapid changes in structure and ecological makeup than many other American wilderness areas, by virtue of history, location and human response. The Adirondacks are unique in that they have allowed climatologists both to assess the impacts of environmental degradation in a contained area and monitor the success of environmental rehabilitation over time. The greatest example to date is the effect of sulfur dioxide, or acid rain, in the park itself. As electric power plants (chiefly coal-fired) spewed sulfur dioxide and nitrous gases from Midwestern facilities, prevailing winds carried the particles, which combined with water vapor and oxygen in the atmosphere to form sulfuric acid, across the continent to fall as acid rain on much of northern New York and neighboring states to its east.

Since 1997, Northeastern grassroots environmental campaigns like Citizens Campaign for the Environment have been fighting to reduce levels of these emissions, to great success. In 2003, the federal EPA introduced new policies to regulate the emissions of dangerous pollutants like sulfur dioxide into the environment; in the last few years, scientists have recorded a significant decrease in atmospheric, aquatic and terrestrial pollutant concentrations within the Adirondack Park. Citizens, along with countless other organizations, continue to promote the health and well being not only of the park but also of those who live within and around it. These groups are the first line of defense against the continued threat of industrial development and pollution within the entire Adirondack region; their value and importance cannot be measured.

February 2007. This semester I applied for and was accepted into St. Lawrence's Outdoor Program guide training course, which every spring selects a handful of university students to participate in and learn from comprehensive wilderness recreation instruction. In addition to the broader course curriculum (wilderness medicine and evacuation, Leave No Trace recreation ethics, trip planning and leadership skills), each student also selects two areas of specialization that focus on specific outdoor activities—in my case, mountaineering and paddling. As part of the training, guide trainees are expected to sacrifice many of their weekends on campus to hone their skills with practical experience in and around the Adirondacks.

On this particular weekend, we have come to summit Algonquin Mountain, the second highest peak in the Adirondacks, inferior in elevation only to Mount Marcy and standing just over five thousand vertical feet. It's been a long morning, and our group of eight has split down the middle, with only four of us continuing up the trail to the top. Below the tree line, weather wasn't much of an issue; pleasant white sunlight filtered through the trees and reflected off mounded snow banks while flakes sifted down silently from the loaded branches above. We've focused on the technical aspects of the climb, the ice steppes and rock walls too tricky to bypass without stopping to strap on our crampons. We push steadily forward, determined to summit. The trail up Algonquin is not difficult; the path follows a gradual incline that shadows the route of an alpine stream as it wends its way downhill to join the watershed. The steady slope has made the trek gentle, despite the aforementioned rough patches—that is, until we clear the trees.

As we emerge on top of the ridge, our world is instantly transformed. What seem like gale-force winds race downward from the summit, whistling around us as they diverge against the spiny ridgeline, thoroughly assaulting us, cutting through our many layers of Gortex and polypro, hurling fine, pricking ice grains against our faces until I have no feeling left above my neck. It is at least another half mile or more to the summit; we press onward, heads bent, into the storm. Visibility is nonexistent, and the footing beneath us is hard pack, a thick layer of ice slippery even with crampons. I feel the burn in my quads as the bulk of my weight rests upon them alternately with each ascending footfall. I find myself utterly humbled by this mountain, the complexity and technicality of it, and I tell myself to take care as I struggle uphill.

We do not linger at the summit, just long enough to take a few pictures, and though the wind is beyond fierce and we are completely exposed, I take off my pack and remove the one rock I carried with me—the rock that will stay, I hope, until spring, when someone from the Adirondack Nature Conservancy comes to place it in a barrier or as part of a pathway. I noticed the sign at the trailhead encouraging hikers to carry a few stones from the pile to the top of the mountain, in essence to give something back to the mountain. The Nature Conservancy works all year-round in the park, negotiating land sales, educating youngsters and adults alike and preserving the rich heritage of the Adirondacks. The Conservancy also employs educators to work on ecological restoration projects, like re-seeding the summits of Algonquin and comparable mountains—fragile high-alpine ecosystems that have seen an increase in human traffic and therefore endured heavily accelerated erosion. Over time, these systems have begun to recover, but it will take an ongoing commitment by organizations like the Conservancy and demand increased awareness on the part of those who come to these mountains to recreate—everyone must be willing to effect change.

The first book I read that really discussed the Adirondacks in detail was for an environmental literature course during my sophomore year. I had just returned to St. Lawrence from a year's absence when I took a break to re-evaluate my own perspective on things. And when I came back, resolute and determined to be better, it was Bill McKibben's memoir *Wandering Home* that began to inspire a different vision, one that is continuing to evolve today. In his book, McKibben takes a long and thoughtful look at his own landscape by walking through it, ambling from the Green Mountains of Vermont (a decidedly less aggressive environment than the rough-and-tumble North Country) across the boundary formed by Lake Champlain and into the Adirondacks. Along the way he meets with friends new and old, people all in some way actively involved in the ongoing conversation not simply about the state of the environment, but about connectivity, about bringing communities together.

I was touched by his writing, moved by what he wished for this region: that people here might come together, that small communities might thrive and flourish even in so harsh a climate by relying on one another, that local economies could exist and be sustained by a move toward more sustainable practices in agriculture, industry and business. I can't pretend that even as I read his book, at twenty years old, I was remotely aware of the intricacies or implications of a truly "local economy," how one is developed, sustained and proven successful. I'm not sure I do even now. But what I could understand, what struck a deep chord within me, was the importance McKibben placed on the human interactions, of knowing one's place within the context of a greater network and acknowledging that our mutual dependencies actually suggest strength, instead of weakness.

September 2008. I think back to a few weekends ago when I spent a day working with Habitat for Humanity on a one-room log cabin at the Bennett Bittersweet Farm, just off the northwest foothills. The farm is a family operation, about thirty minutes down the highway from campus in the heart of an Amish settlement. It was early when we started that morning, and I was groggy, hung over and not in the least ready to start swinging hammers.

Upon our arrival, we met Brian, the family patriarch, and his wife, Ann. Before we started work, Brian insisted on letting us mosey around the property, saying hello to the animals, talking to us about his land and his vision for the future. Bittersweet is a small-scale, organic operation; the farm produces mixed and specialty vegetable crops, chicken eggs and broilers, hogs, sheep and turkeys. The animals are heritage breeds, and the produce are heirloom varieties, meaning the Bennetts are doing all they can to promote and sustain biodiversity in this difficult and unforgiving landscape.

I extricate myself from the group and cross the path to see the hogs. They are Tamworths, displaying the traditional russet hue of their breed. They are friendly and inquisitive, pressing their muddy, flaring snouts to my fingertips as their bright, brown eyes search my face and their companions root through the swill of the enclosure—they couldn't be happier.

The turkeys next door are somewhat less excited about the prospect of a human encounter and send up an unnecessary ruckus at my approach. I lean casually against the fence watching these mammoth specimens strut their stuff, deciding they look more like weird ornamental plants than birds with their rows of speckled plumage erupting from all sides.

I move down the fence row and say a quiet hello to the chicks who were hatched just days ago, who lie warm and still in sawdust under heat lamps, piled on top of one another, spilling over with tiny wing-nubs splayed into the nooks and crannies created by their neighbors. Their incessant peeping creates a perpetual hum, and the entire downy soft mass of them seems to me like one gently throbbing organism—they are alive together, and fragile, and suddenly I am ready to go to work.

We worked for several hours that day, helping to raise the cabin where I would, one year later, sit and discuss literature on sustainable agriculture as part of my local food course. I didn't know it at the time, but I was helping to build and create a community that would benefit me personally and continue to benefit others for a long time to come. When we were finished for the day, the Bennett family sent us home with a basket of zebra tomatoes, luscious green orbs just beginning to ripen, threaded with vertical bands of gold, and a carton of umber-hued eggs from the chickens. We didn't ask for anything in return for our work, but they were given in thanks, and somehow knowing that I was helping to keep their farm alive and flourishing made the gesture that much sweeter.

These experiences, and so many others, have led me forward, allowed me to see my place in a greater community. Just as it always has been, this process of growing community and regional awareness is ongoing, and as global climate change and the importance of local connectivity continue to make headlines I find myself ever more thankful for what I have learned.

I believed for a long time that as soon as I graduated, I would rush back to the West Coast with all haste, and perhaps remember fondly but with detachment the time I spent in the North Country. But it's different for me now, because I've learned to love that environment for so many reasons. I found myself there, with the people, and in the mannerisms and culture that have largely informed my perspective on land stewardship and environmental ethics. No matter where I go in my life, there will always be a pull, a gentle tug on my heartstrings that calls me back to the Pacific Northwest. I think most people probably feel that way about their home. It's a natural comfort. But wherever I find myself down the line, I will be using the knowledge that began to grow and develop in the North Country: a set of skills both practical and theoretical that I hope will keep me in good stead. And of course, there is a part of me that will always be a little bit homesick for the Adirondack North Country—it is, after all, where I grew up.

Part III

The Flora and the Fauna

Left: Tara Freeman.

Below: Betsy Tisdale.

Left: Whiteface Hurrah. *Deb Kanze.*

Below: Whiteface Mountain (left center) and the McKenzie Range from Donnelly's Corners. *Debbie Kanze.*

Betsy Tisdale.

Debbie Kanze.

Debbie Kanze.

Elizabeth Johnston Hubbard.

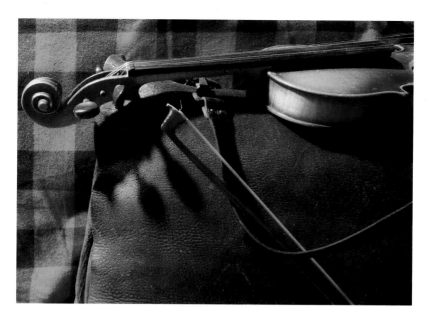

Harry's Mail Pouch. *Dan Berggren.*

Dan Berggren. *Jessica Riehl.*

Left: *Life Cycle. Tim Fortune.*

Below: *Green Frog. Tim Fortune.*

Right: Matt Carpenter.

Below: Barry Lobdell.

Barry Lobdell.

Algonquin Mountain and the McIntyre Range. *Henning Vahlenkamp.*

Algonquin Mountain and other High Peaks of the Adirondacks. *Henning Vahlenkamp.*

Jean Williams-Bergen.

Left: Jean Williams-Bergen.

Below: Deb MacKenzie.

Right: Jean Williams-Bergen.

Below: Deb MacKenzie.

Jim Bullard.

Eastern Screech Owl. *Brian Henry.*

Above: Northern
Hawk Owl.
Brian Henry.

Right: Ermine.
Kevin MacKenzie.

Above: Dix Mountain. *Kevin MacKenzie.*

Left: *Kevin MacKenzie.*

Above: *Kevin MacKenzie.*

Right: The Great Ice Storm of 1998. *Mark Kurtz.*

Mount Colden. *Kevin MacKenzie.*

ADIRONDACK GOAT BOY

By Jonathan Collier

The rumen, the reticulum, the abomasums, the omasum. The four stomachs of a goat. Growing up on a goat farm in northern New York guaranteed that I was the only kid in school capable of reeling off any number of goat-related facts and tidbits. Instead of playing football or hockey on the weekends, I spent my time caring for and learning about the art of goat herding.

People have often asked me when or why I decided to raise and work with this particularly stubborn variety of livestock. I can't say that I've ever had anything other than a simple answer to that question: until I was sixteen or seventeen years old, my parents owned a goat that was older than I was.

So many of my earliest memories involve going out to the barn and taking care of the animals. When I was younger, this was, as far as I could tell, the worst part of getting home from school at night. Instead of watching TV or playing a video game like my friends normally spent their evenings, it was fill up two grain pans with Coarse 14 and one pan with Caprine goat grain and then put another scoop in the milk stand for later. After a fight with the goats to get the grain into their stall without spilling it, hay would need to be taken out to the pasture—two bales in winter and one bale during the short, almost unnoticed stretch of North Country summer. During the arctic winter, there would be (frozen) water buckets to empty and refill. This task tended to be particularly unpleasant when the temperature dropped to twenty-five or more below zero. On the flipside, I became quite accustomed to frigid temperatures in nothing but jeans and a sweatshirt, a skill that has proved invaluable on a number of occasions, as I've never owned a car. And of course, we almost always had at least one doe, or female goat, in milk during the year. As far as I know, I am the only student in my graduating class who knew how to milk an animal, let alone drink anything other than cow's milk. But I'll come back to the milk later on.

One drawback to being the only goat farmer my age in the Saranac Lake area was that I acquired a nickname. Goat Boy. While some friends and family used the term affectionately, it was also an easy opportunity for some of my less wholesome classmates to pick and tease. One particular instance that I will always remember occurred when I was in the eighth grade. I had recently attended a fundraiser for a local animal shelter, bringing a couple of my goats along to entertain the younger children. Since I was the only person at the fundraiser with goats, a picture of me and one of the goats ended up in the newspaper the following day. Unfortunately, my English teacher noticed it and devised what he thought was a wonderful activity for some class participation and creative expression. Much to my dismay, I arrived at class to discover him handing out photocopies of my picture from the paper for a caption contest. Each student would write down a caption for the photo, then he would read them aloud to the class and they would decide which was the most humorous. Needless to say, my teacher read four or five before realizing that at least half of the captions would be entirely inappropriate to read aloud in an eighth-grade English class and threw them in the recycling bin.

When I was a bit older, and beginning to appreciate the experiences of owning livestock and working with animals, the goats took on a more important role in my life. After a forgettable seven- or eight-month stint with the Boy Scouts, my parents suggested that I try 4-H. So I joined the "cows and cookies" organization with my goats as my project.

This proved to be one of the most influential choices in my life. While at first I felt a bit out of place as the only kid with goats in my club, I quickly realized that 4-H was about more than what kind of animal you had (if you had any animals at all); it was about anything and everything that might interest someone, about making friends with new people and learning new skills to better myself for the future. I suddenly found myself surrounded by other kids who either had some variety of livestock themselves or didn't think it was weird that I lived on a goat farm. Finding a level of acceptance that I had encountered only a few times before, I dove headlong into my dairy goat projects.

The breed of goat that made up the majority of our herd was the Nubian. Known for high butter fat content, big floppy ears, rounded "Roman" noses and the tastiest milk, Nubians are a desert breed also known for their extreme stubbornness. But I suppose that fit rather well with my Irish heritage, as well as my Adirondack upbringing.

Since Nubians are considered to produce tasty milk, the next logical step was to make something tasty out of that milk. My first project was butter, which probably sounds a bit easier than it actually is. After waiting for the cream to separate, you add in a couple of ingredients and put it in a blender. Or, if you seek a more authentic experience, you put it in a mason jar and proceed to shake the jar vigorously until you start to lose feeling in your arms. I eventually lost track of how many mason jars I shook before I got the recipe just right.

Following my success with butter, I moved on to cheese, which is a much more commonly known use of goats' milk. From cheese curds and cheddar to spreads and feta, you can produce any cheese made with cows' milk. In fact, despite the U.S. obsession with cows, a majority of the rest of the world uses goats as their primary source of milk and meat. From cheese, I progressed to fudge, ice cream and a variety of other delightful snacks.

While researching recipes for cheese and desserts, my dad ran across an interesting note concerning antiques. After delving into it a little deeper, we discovered that most antiques were originally coated with milk paint. Being the spirited goat farmers that we are, we decided to repaint the barn with our extra milk. But of course, living in the middle of the Adirondacks, it took us a fair amount of time to locate a store that actually stocked the ingredients (or one that was willing to order them from a less rural area). After that lengthy search came an even lengthier period of trial and error with the ingredients. In due course, we managed to concoct milk paint in a classic barn red. Dad and I then spent the next couple of weeks, between taking care of the animals and school, repainting our barn a color that the ancient siding probably hadn't seen in well over fifty years. And, seeing as our goat farm isn't much more than a hobby of sorts, any time we're able to use our goats (or their products) in place of things we might otherwise have to purchase, it's a step in the right direction.

Another interesting fact that most people don't know about goats is that they can carry up to 35 percent of their own body weight. While 35 percent might not seem like all that much, if you have a goat that weighs between 200 to 250 pounds or more, you're looking at a fair amount of weight that they can bear. Now I, as any good Adirondacker, have a love of hiking and the outdoors. And (remember, we were enthusiastic goat farmers) my parents and I decided to combine the two interests. We proceeded to practice with the goats, slowly coaxing them to wear packs and saddlebags on their backs, climb over and under obstacles at our command and not chew on the straps. In time, our goats became even more reliable out on the trail than most dogs. Because we hand-raise all of our goats, they are extremely attached to us and don't stray off into the woods the way dogs tend to do. We've also never had to worry about them biting any friendly strangers we meet in the woods.

I'm fairly certain that I complained a lot when I was younger, attempting to get out of doing barn chores at night or avoided going out to the barn for as long as possible in hopes of my parents being done by the time I arrived. I often felt left out of a lot of social circles because I was that kid with the goats. But after twenty-one years of growing up with, raising and caring for my animals, I wouldn't have it any other way. I am Goat Boy, and I am proud of that fact. Except for the caption contest. I'll take a pass on that one for next time.

SIGHTINGS

By Maurice Kenny

In Memory of Lorraine Wilson, friend

It seems a century ago but, in reality, was only a decade, when, walking along a tree-lined street in Manhattan's West Village I observed a large male raccoon sitting on a slender limb. That morning I was on my way to my CPA's office on Greenwich. I stood stunned, my heart racing with excitement. A raccoon…in New York City, the bohemian neighborhood.

It didn't take long to buy at the Eighth Street Bookstore a small paperback on wild animals of New York City. I was on the prowl, on point. Deer, skunk, red-tailed hawks beneath the Brooklyn Bridge, opossums sighted out on Long Island and several parks in the boroughs… Brown bats fly the night skies and Norway rats take up residence in tenements. Great blue herons surprise the eye; the usual squirrels, the peanut-crunching chipmunk, the kitchen mouse and even weasels are there on the daily hunt. I never had the joy of coming upon a red fox, but friends have sighted the gorgeous tail scampering into woody stands. And of course the least endangered beast in New York State, the white-tailed deer. Yes, in the city of New York, Central Park, Queens and the Bronx. Should you doubt these discoveries, consult the book *New York City Wildlife Guide* by Edward R. Ricciuti, published by Shocken Books. A wonder, an absolute delight. The creatures are there.

ONE

Around that time I decided to go home, to northern New York, to visit several friends and have myself a short vacation and eventually sojourn at Owls Head Mountain, near Malone, where at the time the Native American/Mohawk "Akwesasne Notes" was published. I had been publishing many poems in the paper, and Jerry Gamble, the editor, asked if I might come and offer an arm of labor with the staff. I shouted for joy…YES! So I "bundled me bag," as the young Irish girl in *Finian's Rainbow* sang, and started off through the winter by Greyhound bus, first stop Joe and Carol Bruchac's in Greenfield Center, a small village near Saratoga. I spent a delightful afternoon rocking in Carol's kitchen chair close to the potbelly stove while she prepared lunch and talked of their press, the Greenfield Review, and its new publications.

Late that afternoon they were to drive to Onchiota, in the heart of the Adirondacks, to visit John (Kahionhes) and his wife, Eva (Karonhisake) Fadden, their three sons and John's father Ray (Tehanetorens) Fadden, a true historian of Iroquois (Haudenosaunee) culture. Eva gave us a delicious supper; John, a very fine artist, offered to give us a view of his new paintings and drawings; and Ray told us stories.

It was growing late. Joe and Carol needed to be on the road home and still had to drop me north at Owls Head, where Jerry was to meet me at the highway. Shouting and waving fond goodbyes, we left in a rather thick snowstorm, much to the Bruchacs' chagrin. They gathered strength, and we drove on to Tamarack, no more than a bar/restaurant/gas station, and left me off there, as just behind, at the foot of Owls Head Mountain, were the "Notes" offices. Tamarack no longer exists; fire took its breath and life.

The snow ceased, affording my driver/hosts a better trip home. In moments, Jerry was at the door, and we left the place reeking with good smells of steak, homemade french fries and sautéed onions.

We stepped out into the winter night, snow beautifully lit by a huge full moon now uncovered from the storm, and began to climb the mountain in deep snow under the intoxicating smell of pine trees. Jerry took us slowly up, he a few yards ahead of my slow progress—remember, I had been living in Brooklyn Heights, not on a mountaintop.

I felt a presence other than Jerry. I felt a tinge of heat fall against my cheek, or did I simply imagine it? I heard a soft pad of feet not mine in the snow. Finally I had enough sense to open my eyes while stopping to search this odd sensation taking over the night.

There he stood. Solid black in the night. Thick winter fur. The brilliant moonlight pierced through open white pine branches. His yellow eyes sparkled in the pale twilight. He stood ground. Neither of us moved, spoke, breathed. I was frozen. I did not speak, nor did he; neither did he wag his tail nor I raise an arm in fear or friendship. It did not shock or surprise me when quickly he disappeared into the night woods.

I called out to Jerry, "There was a dog following us!"

"No," he replied. "It was not a dog. A wolf."

"Impossible," I blurted out. "They were all shot, killed by the old-time loggers and miners and farmers."

"Not all. There remain a handful. They are rarely spotted. Smart brothers. They know when to appear and when to stay quietly in the den…for obvious reasons. Mankind has not been tolerant or loving toward the wolf. He must slink through life in these Adirondacks. What a shame, what a tragedy."

Wolf is brother to the Mohawk. Jerry stood there contemplating the fate of the great grey wolf in these northern climes.

With Jerry leading the way we ascended to the peak. By oil lamplight I composed a poem and dedicated it to the Bruchacs. The only other animals I saw on that trip into the mountain ranges were house mice in the drawer of a desk, eating stamps, or hanging from the ceiling at night in the cabin office.

Sacrifice

For Joe and Carol

wolf tracks
on the snow
I follow between
tamarack and birch
cross the frozen creek
dried mulleins
with broken arms
stand in shadows
tracks move uphill
deeper into snowed conifers
I hurry to catch up
with his hunger

cedar sing in the night
of the Adirondacks
he huddles under bent
red willow
panting
I strip in the cold
wait for him to approach
he has returned
to the mountains
partridge drum
in the moonlight
under black spruce

Two

Eventually I returned to Brooklyn Heights somewhat longing for the north, the natal waters, the homeland where the placenta was buried at my birth; where a headstone partially reads: "Here Rests…" I could not stay in the city much longer. It was the pull, the almost desperate need to reunite with my heritage, my sense of place, spiritual demands—as Jack London wrote, "the call of the wild." I vacated my brownstone apartment in which I had lived twenty-two years for the Adirondack Mountains, moved into a building called Tamarack House, a students' residence in Saranac Lake, with the intent of teaching as "poet in residence." I remained at North Country Community College for six years. Then other institutions offered positions, and I took off but kept my residence in the mountains, where life bubbles at the moment.

In humor I will say that there in Tamarack House I found some wild animals: college students. Some were absolutely delightful, others scary. One day I saw a young man taking the door off an apartment in which he did not reside. I asked him a simple question: "Why?" His answer: "I'm bored." My thought was: "He's stoned." It was a fun year.

And within that span of time I did find my first true wild animal since moving home. Mice don't count. A friend, a colleague at the college, asked if I'd be interested in taking a ride to Long Lake, forty miles down mountain roads. He needed to take care of some business dealing with boats. Naturally, I jumped into the car, and off we went to a charming village at the midpoint upon a long, thin lake where seaplanes take off and land daily for tourists to view the lay of the land. We drove through the quaint town, turned right and began to climb a hill.

I was astonished. Many years I had heard of a black creature homing in the mountains, 95 percent of the time arboreal, living in the trees of the forest. I sat in my seat gaping at an adult fisher crossing the pavement at a leisurely pace. Fishers are rare in the United States. They belong to the weasel family. Mr. Fisher is touchy. He is not a good pet for children. Don't attempt to pet him, let alone pick him up in your arms, should you come across him in the woodlands.

Naturally, deer filtered in and out of our wildland view, their numbers growing fast since they are threatened by no enemy other than humankind. Bear were constantly talked about, as were moose. Raccoons were in great numbers, by the dozens; several love-traps needed to be on hand. Woodchucks and various moles proliferated; squirrels and red and brown chipmunks were always close.

Some folks in the north call all things—even black flies—"critters." I believe that epithet to be unkind. They deserve our respect. They deserve their proper names.

My next animal was a marvel, such a simple beast, but a gorgeous gift of the Creator: a silver or gray fox. Friends of mine, Jean and John, lived in a small but comfortable cabin near a pond they paddled, where both muskrat and beaver homed. They were fairly common, especially the beaver, which has returned to make new wetlands and ponds for us, though not all of the mountain folks are happy about that. Jean and John were. On a pleasant deck overlooking a wild cranberry bog, they hung bird feeders. All types of birds responded. One day when I was out for a venison dinner accompanied by cooked marsh-marigold leaves, I stared out the window onto the bog and spotted a fantastic unexpected vision. There, against the outside wall, feet on the windowsill, staring through the window at us—humans, strangers, probably enemies but also feeders of birds and beasts so why not take advantage of this lovely gift—was a fox. He returned often to the feeder, yet Jean was worried he would attack her cats, some of whom were aged or sickly. He did not touch a single feline, disappearing on his own, but not before John snapped a photo for me. As he presented it, he announced, "This is your new son." A rarity, fine portent. Since then I have observed, though rarely, the beautiful red tail of the common fox sneaking off into the brush, having failed to trap my Maine coon cat in its teeth.

It has been known that the mountain cat, the painter, has made numerous stops at John and Jean's cranberry bog. They have heard cries and observed where its claws have serrated into nearby trees.

THREE

Bear: bold, brave king of the woods. Nasty, smelly, brush-crushing, house-vandalizing, berry-picker, a hill of fur, fat and mighty, a grub lover, a loner. A creature of story and legend. Feared but respected; shunned yet sought by the hunter. Often found as a rug with its head and teeth exposed, on the floor or wall of a human's study. It is a good feeling to know he's here in the woods. He remains a noble, majestic creature.

In story, one that Ray Fadden has told from Iroquois culture, Bear is the emblem of medicine. Because a mother in the Mohawk Bear Clan gave the Creator, disguised as an old man, a place to rest, water to drink when dry and food to eat when famished, the Creator proclaimed that forever more the Bear Clan would hold the powers of curing as he sent that good mother into the woods and fields to find the herbs and grasses that would be made into the medicines needed by the people.

Ray Fadden (Tehanetorens) became the keeper of bears. He would gather leftover food and garbage from various feeding lots: restaurants, home kitchens, packing plants, wherever food was wasted or thrown out. He took it to the forest animals and particularly the bear. They became in a strange way his children, and he became famed for his altruism, his compassion. At any moment you might find two or three bears in his backyard waiting for the feed.

Years back I came to visit the Fadden family in Onchiota, where Ray presided over a Native American collection of artifacts, the Six Nations Indian Museum; now John's son is the caretaker. With me I brought a friend, a strictly city guy who held some sense of adventure: he liked picking berries. And it was blueberry-picking time. Surrounding the Fadden property were clearings where blueberries could be picked at leisure. I took Josh into those sacred fields and allowed him to pick at will, or until his stomach could hold no more. He stood off from me, picking. Suddenly he rose up from the fruit-heavy plants and called out, "What's this?" I moved to his picking spot and saw a large pile of smelly scat. It was steaming on a very hot afternoon. His face was glowing with discovery. "What is it?" he asked. "I know it's something's scat, but what thing?"

I smiled somewhat smugly and answered, "It's the hot steaming scat of an adult bear who remains somewhere near."

Josh the warrior made a mad rush for the car, shouting, "Come on!"

On numerous occasions I have been in the vicinity of bears. One summer, one came down off the mountain rising from the back of my house in Saranac Lake to dig out grubs, which were increasing in number in the easy earth behind a falling wooden retainer wall. A July night. Muggy. A strange reddish light in the sky. In bed. I felt a beggar in the area, a thief. It smelled badly, harshly of crime. It seemed to have rolled down the mountainside, knocking the brush, witchhopple and such. Glory, did he smell. I could imagine I heard him chomping, thoroughly enjoying his repast, and possibly wondering if he could find a door to smash or window into the house for whatever he might feed upon, cheese, fruit, bacon, anything. And what he might smash, destroy as he once did. Not necessarily *my* bear, but *a* bear attacked the home of two friends while they were away on vacation in California. Their bear did a very good job, an expensive one.

One summer not long ago I was visiting friends on Tupper Lake, not far from home in the mountains. Actually, I was there for a creative writing conference. I have a short fuse, and someone set my firecracker off. I left the dining room for a slow walk. I stood gazing out to the beautiful Tupper Lake. It was twilight. August. Nothing much stirred, bird or beast. The porch was nearly flat to the ground with a thin step, which I took with the notion to have a little hike up the dirt road. Hot, a little muggy, slowly growing into the dark night. The blackberries on the canes had burnt and dried; not much profit in picking them.

Dumb. I was struck dumb. Could not move. Nor speak. Call for help. Help myself. Defend myself. Where was a gun? A hammer. A heavy stick. Something helped me remember I was working on a new collection of magic realism stories. I looked deep into the eyes whose gaze rested on my body, I thought in a treacherous way.

It was a yearling, but large enough, aged enough to tear my flesh to shreds. I could not help but feel his great teeth digging into my chilling flesh. For only a moment we stood facing each other's gaze, neither taking his stare from the other. I waited for the blow. I can't now consider other than he awaited the show, bullet rammed into his brain. No Mama there to offer him aid. Nor a gun. We stared. And his eyes spoke: "Stop writing about me. I don't like it." And I responded through my eyes, "I shall never more make fictions of you."

He circled my stunned figure, casually strolled around the side of the cabin where my fellow writers were taking coffee on the screened porch. I knew he'd tear the screen with his mighty claws and teeth. For angering me they deserved a little scare. Later they said they had not seen a bear. I knew he was not a spirit. I could have pinched him through the thick black hair—he was that close, eight feet from me.

I did finish the collection of stories but never composed another one dealing with bears.

FOUR

"My name is Lucy, and I don't have a place to live," called out a good-sized Maine coon cat.

"Not now, kitty," I replied. I went into Hannah McCormick's office, the veterinarian. The cat followed. "You didn't hear me, mister. My name is Lucy, and I don't have a place to live!"

Hannah explained to the cat that I had just lost in death my fourteen-year-old Sula. She then whispered, "He'll be back for you later." Sure enough I was, within three months, and Lucy came home with me joyfully and happily. She proved to be very valuable in numerous ways: friendship, mouse catching, chipmunk and red squirrel tracking. She carried them into the house morning after morning, sometimes dead as a doornail and sometimes wiggling their tails but acting dead, only to run off into the downstairs bathroom. If they were still living, we captured them in a heavy towel and tossed them back outdoors, only to be brought in the next morning. She was accurate and most determined that she would rid the area of this vermin. She was famed. Neighbors wanted to rent her by the week.

She was a domesticated feline and probably should not be included in this story. However, she did play a large part in the wild animal category...perhaps too much. (She was not a bird killer!) Nights of summer she would sit on the veranda and hiss the deer that had come off the mountain to eat the sweet buds of whatever plant stood as their supper. Perhaps they thought she was a dog as they scampered off, and the buds were safe to bloom.

FIVE

For now I believe the region's ecology is safe within the minds of these various local habitants, and so it should be. The deer that ate my yellow lily buds, sweet and tender though they well might have been, was here first. Or the chipmunk that dug up the tulip bulbs—she too has been here a long time and needs to survive to perpetuate the ecological balance of these wondrous forests, lakes and mountains.

I've not yet had a problem with skunks—holding my breath—or raccoons, except one night when we looked through the plate glass living-room picture window to see a raccoon rocking in the rocker and staring into the lit room. Once more Lucy was on duty; she climbed onto the window's ledge and made noises, and the raccoon fled.

For years, white-tailed deer would wander off Mount Dewey behind the house into the various yards of the neighborhood, meaning many cultured plants had not the slightest chance for survival, especially a forsythia plant given to me as a birthday gift. It stood some five feet. Each year it grows…smaller as the deer's sharp teeth find their tender leaves. In ten years I have never spotted a single blossom yellowing in the dawn. One Sunday afternoon, I looked off the veranda into the brush and pines, and there stood an extremely young spring fawn, its tail brushing off black flies, its eyes lovingly looking up at me as if to say, "I've come to play." My response: "Not in my garden. Call your truant mother and have her take you back up to the mountain. I'm not babysitting today." It spent the afternoon.

Lucy was dead. She had at last found a permanent home on the side of the hill behind the house, a place she wandered and obviously respected and certainly enjoyed.

We are all animals…we forget that at times, when attempting to do away with our wild brothers and sisters—the African lion, the gorilla, the grey wolf, the twilight bat.

The pride of lions is majestic, the howl of the wolf reassuring that all is well in the forest, the thieving of white-tailed deer and chipmunk a chore to the home-owner, but perhaps all this is of import. These insignificant setbacks are temporary misfortunes; surely those hungry creatures are adding something to the survival of all. I can offer forgiveness and understanding. And we do get even sitting to a supper of venison stew cooked in red wine with carrots set on the table beside a bowl of steaming wild rice.

What a shame, what a tragedy that we can't live in harmony with our fellow animals. The lion may need the zebra for survival, as we needed the deer. But it is a great pity, possible extinction.

This morning I ventured out to check the growth of flowers and herbs. Yes, the deer nibbled off those sweet tender buds of the hydrangeas and wiped away the low sugary leaves of a sapling mountain ash. Glory be, they did not touch the forsythia...perhaps too low to stoop for those leaves.

Before Lucy—oh yes, there was a before Lucy—deer ate nearly everything that stood. Once she arrived, thinking they were dogs, she would sit on the highest step of the veranda and growl as though she were also a dog. They would stop chomping and make a fast run out of the yard. She was a champion.

Then came the little sneakers on the flat of the earth, those of the neighborhood rodentia. Except in winter, Lucy teethed into her favorite game: red squirrel and chipmunk, as much a nuisance as the deer. Plant tulip bulbs or daffodil or hyacinth: that same afternoon those bulbs are gone and placed safely away in a den for winter eating. Heavy stones placed over their beds and still the vermin would roll them off and feast. Lucy was extremely valuable.

The beaver has returned. Glorious! The raccoon and mouse and snowshoe hare procreate to this autumnal second!

Bullfrogs galore, porcupine, and not all dead on the pavement. Bobcats (at times called bay lynx) abound in nature's woods. I've seen a few, but patiently wait the first sighting of a moose standing tall in a mossy swamp, off to the side a bald eagle protecting its young high on a white pine branch. I see, hear, and am glad that I can breathe a sigh of relief and know something is good in Creation's world.

The red-tailed hawk eyeing its mouse-breakfast attests to the fact that the journey forward will be enjoyable and safe. He is a fine fetish to have.

⟐

The raccoon in Greenwich Village started my interest in the wild animals of the Adirondacks, and it was again a raccoon that peered into our living room and took the mouse. One day, I went out to pull weeds from the garden. Purple vetch was invading maliciously. Up the driveway, quite close to the garage door, rested in silence a dead grey kitchen mouse. I don't usually come upon such things, but there he was, and I believed newly dead. No more Lucy alive to do it, and not the current queen cat, Elesse, who is not allowed outdoors because of the heavy traffic on our mountain road.

I nudged it with my foot, thinking it was playing dead to fool me. It did not react to my shoe. I walked off. The next morning I found the mouse missing. In the night, a raccoon probably came off the mountain and swept away the deceased rodent. That gave me a special thrill; its death was not in vain. It had fed something.

Now. My work is done, my writing has come to a close. Imagine this, while I'm typing here at the machine the song of a mourning dove draws my attention to the second-floor balcony. I casually stroll out and look over the railing. There, racing across my green yard, is a black squirrel. I have never seen this creature before in Saranac Lake. I thought they stayed in the lower provinces of Canada. Who imported this animal? A boat like the one that brought the Norway rat! Well, I was excited. I cleared my throat, and the sound frightened the little beast and it ran off into the brush.

Lucy couldn't help. Lucy died by poisoning. She was poisoned by a neighbor.

BOGS, BERRIES AND BEYOND

By John Radigan

There is more than one path into the future.
—Helena Norberg-Hodge

Adirondack bogs are mysterious, enigmatic, vaguely sinister places where exotic species like red pitcher plants and leatherleaf, orchids and carnivorous sundews, share space with thick undulating mats of mint green sphagnum moss and mournful stands of stunted cedars. The acidic black waters underneath, which nearly claimed my dog's life one summer day long ago, seem bottomless, inhabited mainly by the occasional snapping turtle in its prehistoric gray-green armor. Masses of submerged rotting vegetation give off a heavy sulfurous stench when the surface of those cold depths is disturbed. The bog is a kind of no-man's land, existing in the interstitial space between solid and liquid, not quite one, not quite the other. It is amorphous, ever-shifting, surreal. It represents, writes Cherrie Corey, "primordial beginnings, dark repositories of death and rebirth, landscapes of mystery and intrigue."

For over a decade, I lived beside such a bog, in a cottage perched high above it on a sandy esker in Coreys, near Tupper Lake, New York. Like the terrain below, the cottage itself had an uneasy foot in two worlds simultaneously. Originally built as a summer cottage by Ross Freeman, one of the first licensed Adirondack guides, it was only partially winterized. The crawl space underneath provided none of the weatherproofing of a basement, and in the depths of January, the floor inside could become cold enough to freeze the water in the cat's dish solid a mere three feet from the struggling woodstove. Meanwhile, this shadowy undercroft provided a cold-weather haven for numerous small animals over the years. Most memorable of these one season was a beautiful silver fox, who engaged in regular snarling matches with the pets when they ventured out in the evenings and who appeared like clockwork on the deck every morning barking his demand for a breakfast handout at the living-room window.

But despite the rigors that living there entailed, the place had charm. I had fallen in love with it on my first visit years before I came to live there, drawn in by the warmth of the wood fire, the old-fashioned coffeepot on the small gas range in the kitchen, the lovingly oiled hunting rifles in the gun rack on the wall, the red-and-black checked coats hanging on the peg by the front door, the stars blazing through the canopy of balsams outside over the porch. When, much later, after I had come to stay, a bedroom wing was added and the living room was opened up, the space became even more enchanting, full of light from the new picture window, the hip roof gently supported from inside by a tall, smoothly peeled cedar tree trunk that glowed golden in the afternoon sunshine. From the very beginning, everything about that little place spoke to me of a slower-paced human-scale way of life that even then was under threat from the forces of change gathering momentum out beyond the borders of the Blue Line.

How strange it seems to reflect on all this in a world full of cable TV and computers and iPods, the Internet and cell phones bouncing their signals off satellites positioned out in space—to realize that I, like the bog, also have a foot, so to speak, in two incompatible worlds, that I too inhabit an interstitial space, a kind of shadow land where I can be fully in neither one realm nor the other.

Of course one cannot live for very long beside a bog without thinking cranberries. So early on in my stay, I decided to plant some and to see if I could manage to harvest a crop. After investigating, I found out that a special hardy strain of cranberry plants was available at the St. Lawrence Nursery between Madrid (stress on the first syllable, MAD-rid, if you please!) and Potsdam. So I made the trip and was greeted by Bill, the proprietor, a lean suntanned character wearing a kepi reminiscent of the one Buster Crabbe used to sport in the old TV series about the French Foreign Legion. It turned out that he, like me, was indeed a foreigner, an import, to the North Country and had been one of my classmates at Harpur College near Binghamton many years previously. After much reminiscing and as much of talking business as we needed, I came away with an old cardboard box full of tough brown tangled little shoots which, I had been assured, would take well to the new home I had in mind for them.

Setting them out was, to say the least, something of an adventure. To begin with, it was mid-May and the first wave of the legendary Adirondack blackflies was out in force. After just a few minutes under the ever-strengthening sun, my scalp was a mass of bloody crusts, and thin crimson trickles were making their way down my forearms and bare ankles as clouds of the tiny insects feasted to their hearts' content. There was nothing much to do but put up with it. I had figured out through prior experimentation that hats or, even worse, those fine-mesh olive drab bug helmets they sell to tourists at all the camp stores were virtually useless against the onslaught. A few of the cursed things would always find their way in somewhere, at which point things would become really grim, like being locked in a cell with a microscopic Charles Manson.

Keeping one's footing was also tricky. Even hugging the edge of the bog, it was easy to step off suddenly into two feet or so of bitter dark water, stirring up a whiff of sulfur and more often than not getting a nasty gouge on the calf from a prickly leatherleaf plant or errant broken branch just under the surface. To top everything off, the work was surprisingly, agonizingly, slow. Never having attempted anything remotely like this before, I had only the dimmest idea of whether I was in fact setting out the shoots properly or not. It seemed that Bill's hasty run-through of the procedure as I was paying for the box down in the St. Lawrence valley had pretty much taken flight. I was especially concerned, as I looked back over the territory I had covered, to notice that I couldn't actually tell where the new plants really were. As soon as my hands left them, they had blended seamlessly into the tangled vegetation fiercely asserting itself in that alien terrain.

After several hours of this, the cardboard box was finally empty. Sweaty, stained with bog water and bloody from uncountable fly bites and scratches, I stumbled back up to the top of the esker, popped open a Molson's, cleaned myself up as best I could and settled in for what I knew would be a long period of waiting.

The Celts believe that there are certain places on the planet where the barrier between the physical and the spiritual thins to almost nothing, providing access to perceptions beyond those common in ordinary life. Surely the bog below my cottage was one such place. As the peepers quieted and spring flowed into summer, I found myself drawn more and more frequently to its undulating surface and otherworldly appearance, the shrill whine of its mosquitoes, the powerful croaking of its bullfrogs that echoed from its steep sandy banks in the summer twilight. There was something oddly timeless about its expanse, something that made whatever might be going on in the rest of the world seem all but irrelevant. Walking anywhere near the bog, even on the gray weathered planks I had anchored with chain to each shore, brought a queasy sense of vulnerability. We urbanized westerners often forget how subject we are to the forces of the natural world, believing that we are independent of them or that we can override them by our cleverness and technology. One can have no such illusions here. Most plants cannot grow in this environment, made acidic by the sphagnum with its hollow stems. What soil there is is poor in nutrients, and oxygen levels are low. The whole place reeks of *duende*, the knife-edge between life and death, for sphagnum is slow to rot, and dead matter remains attached to the living plants, forming spongy mats of peat that can accumulate for centuries. Even things of beauty, like the sundews and the pitcher plants in their delicate shades of green and pink, conceal lethal threats. I still remember the panic in my dog's eyes as she clung one afternoon to the edge of a sphagnum mat, back legs thrashing in the brown water searching desperately for a way to pull herself up to safety. Had I not been there, I am sure she would have slipped in and quickly drowned. In this place, one could see displayed a metaphor for the rigors every living thing faces in its struggle to survive on this tiny speck of planet whirling in the hostile immensities of the universe.

In light of all this, I was naturally concerned for the fate of my little cranberry plants and anxiously kept my eye out for signs that they had somehow beaten the odds and taken hold. But by now they had so well blended in that the task was impossible. No matter how hard I looked, they were indistinguishable from the leatherleaf and other vegetation. I took this as a good sign. And I began to reflect that they were a lot like I was—imported from a different locale, planted here in the midst of an unforgiving wilderness and, by some miraculous means, adapting so well to their new surroundings that they had integrated seamlessly as though they had been there for generations. I, too, had arrived here in the rugged Adirondack landscape, with my wool pants and Bean boots and gray Nissan pickup truck with the door latches that froze into inoperability at thirty-eight degrees below zero, and had come to feel at home with the snow covering the fresh daffodils on early May mornings and the "who hoots for you?" call of the barred owls deep in the balsams. I, too, had made a home here in this place at once so inhospitable and so beguiling. This place where the tough granite and slippery black mud of physical reality thin out to evanescence in the tranquil glow of a full moon over Follensby Pond and the echoing tremolo of a loon in some deep-shadowed bay. Part of me knows that I live in a twenty-first-century world of Wal-Mart, globalization, Mideast wars and the Super Bowl. Like everyone else in America, I drive the highways here at a mile a minute, always on my way to somewhere. But a part also clings to this primordial landscape that takes things slow, where the painted trilliums bloom in their own time and the ice goes out in the spring when it damn well pleases.

This, to be sure, is a kind of double-mindedness, and the Bible warns us that "a double-minded man is unstable in all his ways" (James 1:8). Certainly a lack of necessary focus can often be the occasion for trouble or even disaster. But sometimes I wonder whether a degree of such double-mindedness may not be a blessing, like having two eyes, with the stereoscopic vision they permit, or two legs with the resulting capacity for balance and locomotion. Having a foot in both worlds is not necessarily a bad thing. It enlarges our sense of reality and prevents us from falling into a narrow sectarianism or rigid ideology; it aids us in becoming more tolerant, more welcoming of divergent points of view. A bog speaks of all this, being neither quite solid ground nor really a body of water, an environment that harkens back to an earlier geologic era yet suffers from the harmful effects of modern-day climate change.

As summer wore on into early autumn, I began to realize that no crop would be forthcoming this season. Maybe it was, I told myself, just the result of the inevitable period of adjustment to a new environment. Surely there would be berries next year when the plants had recovered from their relocation around the edges of the bog.

I reassured myself in this belief by reflecting that all growth takes place on the edges, on the margins, not at the center. In a tree trunk, the core is dead, while each year's new rings are laid down by the thin cambium layer just beneath the bark. That same potential for new and expanded life is also found among those who live in remote areas like these Adirondacks. It can be seen in people like my friend Kyle living like Ernest Shackleton in his big canvas tent in the winter woods on the outskirts of Saranac Lake. It glows in my friend Bob rereading *Faust* beside his wood fire in his hand-built home on a Bloomingdale hilltop. It is here, among people like this, that the modern world grows thin as cambium and attenuates, and we glimpse something elemental behind and beneath it.

Octavio Paz, the late Mexican poet and winner of the 1990 Nobel Prize for Literature, once wrote that "universality means plurality." On this basis, he built a tremendous edifice of what the critic Pablo Medina has called "cosmic poetry," which takes in, as far as that is possible, the whole world. I think, for example, of his wonderful poem "A Fable of Joan Miro," with its exuberant catalogs of "butterflies, flying fish, wheezing phonographs…the swallow's flash, the foliage of the clouds." Paz's arresting insight is a much later echo of Albert Schweitzer's powerful image of the sea in *The Philosophy of Civilization*: "Just as the wave cannot exist for itself, but is ever a part of the heaving surface of the ocean, so must I never live my life for itself, but always in the experience of what is going on around me."

It is good to remind ourselves occasionally that the Greek root of our word "idiot" is *idiotes*—"a private person," someone who thinks of himself or herself as a wave detached from and independent of the whole in the same way that Dante's sinners become increasingly isolated as we move further and further into the depths of the *Inferno*. The bog I lived beside for over a decade, with its plethora of plant species and complex interconnected ecosystem, taught me much about that same cosmic perspective of universality in diversity. Nothing much really stands out in a bog. Even the cedar trees seem deferential, stunted so as not to tower unduly over the lowlier vegetation. Such egalitarianism, bred of a harsh environment, is more and more a lesson we need to take to heart as we move together, all of us, into an always-uncertain future.

And my little bog reminds us of other truths as well. Its relatively small size, for instance, brings to mind one of the central conflicts of the present age, not between civilization and terrorism or between democracy and dictatorship but between small human-scale local communities and huge impersonal global institutions. The epigraph to this essay comes from Helena Norberg-Hodge's *Ancient Futures: Learning from Ladakh*, which stresses the crucial importance of reweaving "a human, social, and economic fabric that is in harmony with the environment and with human nature." That this idea is gathering momentum as we watch the melting down of so many long-respected systems and institutions is evidenced also in the work of Bill McKibben, the 2008 Conservationist of the Year, who has forcefully challenged the premise that "more equals better" and, in his recent book *Deep Economy*, provides us with a compelling vision of a different kind of future based on community and small-scale human interaction.

David Korten's observation that the shift from a culture based on a love of money to a culture based on a love of life constitutes "the great work of our time" provides us with a final lesson to be learned from the bog at the base of the Coreys esker. I never did harvest any cranberries from all my efforts. Many would therefore count that whole project a failure; I came out at the end with nothing tangible to show for it. The cranberry plants I put in, in other words, were, to such people, merely instruments for producing fruit. We often reduce human beings in a similar way. Our schools largely teach students, for example, to be good employees, ignoring the fact that they have a wider intrinsic worth beyond their economic one. We seek to reform health care not to keep people well but to relieve the cost burden on employers so that we can "create jobs." A while ago I read an account of a protest by migrant tomato pickers against exploitive practices by the growers, a protest that was dismissed by one representative of management with the words "the tractor doesn't tell the farmer how to run the farm." My experience with the bog calls us to look beyond this narrow utilitarian calculus and to see life as valuable simply because it is life.

And so the bog speaks to us of an alternate road, probably the only truly viable one, to a livable human future. It calls us in the direction of community, of small scale, of being part of a larger organic whole. It calls us to remain open to many worlds and to remember our place in a planetary environment that is becoming increasingly harsh and unforgiving. "It is the bog in our brain and bowels, the primitive vigor of nature in us," as Thoreau wrote in August 1856, that inspires our dreams.

THE BLUE BEAR

By Christopher Shaw

The other day a friend told me that, years before, I had given her a gift. We were standing in late afternoon on the steps of my house in a Vermont village, on a day of shifting light and shadow. It was the twenties of November. "I had been complaining about how much I hated November," she said, "and you told me you loved the light. I never looked at November the same way again." The sun fell below the cloud deck and beamed with weak intensity on the west-facing cliffs to the south. I didn't remember saying it, but I definitely agreed with her right then.

I must have been remembering November afternoons in my late twenties, I said, in the Adirondacks, before I gave up hunting. The leaves would have fallen from the hardwoods, exposing the stark bones of the landscape and hazy blue-gray views, usually screened by leaves, extending into the distance. I hunted alone. After mid-month or so, when it got colder, there might be tracking snow, but most of the hunters had traveled to the easier pickings of late season in the southern tier. By then the bucks were insane with hormones, drooling, careless, leaving hysterical scrapes and rubs all over the higher slopes, tearing apart groves of striped maple or birch saplings with their antlers. Tracking, you could try to predict their routes, circle around and intercept them or approach slowly to catch them *in flagrante*, as I did once a shy doe with a gray muzzled eleven-pointer that I shot.

Days like that sharpened the senses and turned off the internal conversation. You had to be acute for hours at a time and became absorbed easily. Shifting gears, maybe after realizing that I had strayed far enough to make it hard getting home before dark, the intensity of hunting concentration turned into stillness and immediacy. A stain of pale peach or violet would shade a gray hardwood slope or rock face, or weightless parachutes of snow would drift under a gauzy film of cloud and the diffuse light that you could almost but not quite see blazing on the other side.

On moments like this I first realized the landscape didn't show its original face until late November, when things were ending, when the sun went away and stopped the sap in the trees. The fair-weather migrants and breeders, the all-winter snoozers, had disappeared—the bears, chipmunks, white-throats, hermit thrushes—as if they never existed. Only the chickadees, red squirrels and corvids persisted: the irritable complainers and elusive tricksters. But in leaving, in their absence, those other species pointed to the season's real meaning. The emptiness, the leaving, the turning inward. Everything was leaving, contracting, ending.

It reflected the winding down of the aging process, the contraction of the northern hemisphere's light and biology. The Iroquois had it right. Dreams came thicker in those longer nights, and with the body sheltered from the outer world for extended periods, the inner world of the mind stood forth bright and clear.

One recent November I went to my own forest retreat—a small cabin with no plumbing or electricity, on a remote stretch of the Saranacs—to see if I could get a little closer to the landscape's original face. I was working on a book about how place gave rise to consciousness, having felt over my fifty-year adult experience that place, this place, the Adirondacks, was trying to show me something, something that I still needed to experience directly, unfiltered. If I could do it, it might show me the kind of subjective experience that people would have had of Paleolithic Europe, for instance, with its cold, arid grasslands and migrating reindeer, or the southern coast of Africa in the middle stone age, where people were just figuring out how to eat shellfish and tortoises and, possibly, killing larger game, two places where we had material evidence of the earliest symbolic expression in design, art and technology. Somewhere in there, I believed, the thing we call consciousness had become separated from what we call the world, with a bewildering cascade of consequences.

I had a few days off from work. No road led to the cabin, and our boat was stored for the winter. I canoed across the lake, planning to survive on water, cider, tea, chicken broth and pumpkin seeds, maybe less, for at least three days. I would neither play the radio nor write and would read only after getting into bed at the end of the day. Otherwise I would meditate, sweat in the sauna and work or explore outside.

In the cabin a weasel had cleared out the mice, and chickadees scolded me for not being there at this critical season of survival. I started the fire in the cabin and, in the sauna, took out my cushion and sat, facing through the balsams toward the marsh between the shore and the lake. Low clouds obscured the mountains, the temperature was in the thirties, the northwest wind raw. Birch and maple leaves littered the ground, opening up the view and admitting pale light through the understory.

The anglers and other camp dwellers had fled. One year-round neighbor was taking care of an ailing mother in the village and another his dying father. The gunfire and internal combustion had gone with them, like the birds, though a last plaintive and muted loon call occasionally carried over the wind.

That evening I took a sauna. The next day I alternated meditating for an hour and working around camp or canoeing for an hour. I split and stacked firewood and dropped a couple of maples for next year's fuel.

By the middle of the second day I had lost the feeling of gnawing hunger and felt light, sharp and deliberate in motion. Thoughts of home and work fell away, along with most other thoughts. In the cabin, no motors or whirring mechanical innards competed with the sound of the fire ticking and the distant crows.

I took another long sauna as the cloudy afternoon went from gray to black, going in and out, alternating heat and cold for as long as I could. The firelight on the interior logs and motion of the balsams in the wind made my body and the logs and the trees themselves feel tenuous and fluid. Time seemed more a vertical column of conditioned events all playing out at once than a horizontal line of temporal progression. Previous eras of experience telescoped into view. At night, coyotes called within a few feet of the cabin, close enough that I could distinguish male, female and two adolescent pups.

By the middle of the third day, the feeling of lightness and precision remained but had turned into slow motion and 3-D. Everything magnified, clarified. I sat for hours without a break, empty, a conduit for the voices of crows, ravens and blue jays.

In the deepening silence, the resident species gathered. Faces leered from the creaking tree trunks. At times like these, False Face Society initiates, having fasted and danced and indulged other mind-altering practices, would see and carve the faces free from the trunks, then wear them as masks to dance, heal the sick and sanctify the mid-winter celebration.

That night, my third, the ground froze and a film of snow made the hill slick between the cabin, the sauna and the dock. By midday I hadn't had a thought or written a word for forty-eight hours. When not sitting or sweating, I split firewood and tended fires. When I sat, the breeze, the play of light on the water, the wood smoke, the brightness behind my eyelids, all the sense impressions of my body got blurry and ran together. Nothing separated "me" from the bog, the lake beyond it or the Western High Peaks Wilderness at my back.

Toward dusk the trees groaned in the wind, and faces leered from trunks. As I cooled on the deck between sweats, a motion in my right peripheral vision caught my attention—a golden-crowned kinglet perched in a balsam two feet from my right eye, driven down from the high dwarf conifers by snow and ice. I felt its breathing and heartbeat and heard the words, "There is no point of view in nature." The bog, the fish in its shallow channels, the turtles settling into the mud, the eagle perched in the pine on the point, the loon with its shamanic overtones floated together on a plane with no perspective, no north or south, up or down, like the animal representations I had seen painted on hides or cave walls.

I sat there a long time, the kinglet at my side, following the cold's slow advance from my skin to my core. The wind blew in my face out of the northwest, the approximate direction of Hudson Bay. Out over the lake, a mile or so away, a blue bear hovered over the water in a half lotus, the wind blowing its long guard hairs into wavy curls.

This was not the two- or three-year-old male that had visited the bird feeder in June. That bear had been jet black with no trace of brown, even on its muzzle or brows, a black that sucked light into its vortex along with all your reactions and interpretations. He stood upright ten feet from the cabin's back door, exposing his impressive ursine package and turning his muzzle sideways, using his paw and tongue to shovel sunflower seeds into his mouth. I watched from the rear stoop, just outside the door. Our eyes locked and stayed locked. I breathed and concentrated instead of thinking about it or planning this essay before the experience even played itself out, pouring concentration on him to sear it into memory. But he was overbold. Eventually by clapping and pretending to throw things I persuaded him to leave.

Visions were probably common among people whose capacity for spoken language and symbolic expression was just emerging, 150,000 to 50,000 years ago in Africa and Eurasia, especially when they were sick or close to starvation or death. Such circumstances probably produced the first inklings of spirituality and the sacred, of a "beyond" with meaning. Later the experience became codified in rites of passage. The seeker went "on the hill" for three or four days without food, water or sleep. Singing, chanting and perhaps eating psychotropic plants, he eventually met the animal helper or vision that would help guide decisions and protect family and tribe for the rest of his life. Often the vision found material expression on a rock wall or cave or in a hand-held figurine. In the northern hemisphere, especially among the Sami, Kamchatkan, Ainu, Alaskan and Athabaskan people, bears and loons were among the commonest animal helpers.

In Japanese Zen, visions that arise in the course of extended meditation are called makyo. The practitioner ignores them to avoid being attracted or repelled and distracted from the path to enlightenment. They belong to the realm of powers, called in Sanskrit *Sambogakaya*, intermediate between the consensual reality of everyday life and the non-dual, non-conditioned reality of the liberated state, called *Dharmakaya*. Makyo did, however, mean you were on the right track.

Sambogakaya was the otherworld or place of ancestors visited by shamans, sorcerers and other pre-agricultural people faced with extraordinary choices. It still rises in us in times of stress, drug or near-death experience and may have been easily at hand for people in a world with simple technology and no illusion of certainty. As David Abram says, we hear voices and see visions when reading a book. Similar cognitive experiences would have attended preliterate people reading the signs of nature in a landscape. Their awareness was as embedded in the immediate surroundings, the world outside their bodies, as ours is in work, electronics, internal conversation. They knew that to reach out and embrace the vision, to desire or fear it, was to lose the image, to make it blur and fade back into the conditions that produced it. It gained solidity only through calm attention and concentration, and they knew how to make that happen. For me, all it had taken was three days without food, electronics, sex, motors or mechanical sounds and extended exposure to heat and cold, conditions that would have been common to the pre-colonial inhabitants of the lake, especially during November's steepening slide into seasonal contraction and death.

The blue bear hovered over mid-lake, growing, gaining focus and clarity. In color and sitting posture, in fact, it might have resembled certain Tibetan thangka paintings I had seen. Yet it was three-dimensional, serene but fierce, and by all means there.

My faculties were sound, as far as I could tell. I wasn't crazy. My breath was smooth and slow, the wind in my face. We regarded each other. Then the bear rushed forward in an explosive burst, still in the half lotus position, driven across the lake by the wind, long guard hairs twirling. My pulse increased, but I didn't look away, instead pouring attention on him as I had the all-black macho that June. His gaze bore into me as his body overwhelmed and rushed through mine with a cold blast that finally penetrated my core and blew me out like a candle flame.

RIVERS

By Neal Burdick

By the banks of the sweet Saranac,
Where its limpid waters flow…
—From the Adirondack folk song "Once More a' Lumbering Go"

In all the world there is only one river, and we are part of it. All water is the same, and the same water flows from clouds to brooks to ponds to rivers to oceans and back to clouds, falling on Earth, flowing, evaporating and falling on Earth again in the timeless hydrologic cycle: one river.

I grew up a short walk from where one vein of this universal river meets a lake. As a boy I would try to pin my eyes to a single patch of Saranac River water as it slid into voracious Lake Champlain and wonder where it had come from, and how long it had taken to reach me, and what happened to it as it melted before my eyes into the vastness of the lake. Someone, perhaps one of my parents, patiently explained that it came down from Saranac Lake, on the fringe of my childhood world of reference. Once I learned of the hydrologic cycle, though, I realized my patch of water was an assemblage of many parts that had come from much farther away and would pass by me again someday, and was comforted. And when finally I came to comprehend that we live out our own cycles, I saw that we are one with water.

I learned in school that our bodies are nearly two-thirds water. Each cell bears the chemistry, the memory, of water. As my cosmos expanded, I understood that we are more than merely physically akin to water. "My soul has grown deep like the rivers," wrote the poet Langston Hughes in "The Negro Speaks of Rivers." Geologists tell us that rivers are the prime shapers of Earth's surface; they are shapers of us as well. Trillions of gallons of water are flowing through all the channels of the world's one river at each moment—at this moment—but we can hold a drop on our fingertips. That drop is us.

As it tumbled from the Adirondack highlands to the Champlain Valley floor, the Saranac River of my youth may not have been sweet or limpid, subject as it was to farm runoff, logging debris, municipal waste and paper mill discharge, but it was and remains my natal water, and thus it remains part of me, and I of it. My first ventures from my home, three blocks from the river in downtown Plattsburgh, without the guidance of my mother's protecting hand, took me to the foot of a granite monument commemorating the American victory on land and lake over the British in September 1814. From there I could watch the river water glide reliably, satisfyingly toward the lake and wonder if the soldiers in that battle saw the same water that I did, perhaps the last thing some of them saw before they died.

The river flows under the D&H Railroad bridge moments before melding with the lake; trains would rumble over that bridge, long freights and shining passenger trains, and I would wonder what was in the boxcars and who was in the coaches and sleepers and the dining car, and where they had come from and where they were going, and why, and whether they were part of some great intangible cycle too. How long did they take to reach me, and would they pass by me again one day, here or somewhere else? Was I part of them, and they of me?

A friend, a biology professor with a streak of philosopher, says we must all seek the headwaters of the river nearest our home, nearest our roots, and follow that river to its conclusion, not in a car along convenient roads, separated from it, but on foot or in a vessel. We must become one with it. For only then will we begin to know where we have come from, and where we are going, and where we fit in the great cycle. My Saranac collects the fallen rains and snows of the northern Adirondacks and then carries them through forests, past hamlets, along farm fields and over dams, down into the Champlain Valley before blending them into Lake Champlain, where it rides the currents into the St. Lawrence River and on to the Atlantic Ocean before returning to the sky to carry the cycle on. This is who I am.

Heraclitus, the Greek philosopher, said, "You cannot step into the same river twice," meaning nothing stays the same. That may be true superficially, but the fundamental cycle continues, always in flux but in superficial ways. It is bigger than we are. We may never intercept it at the same point—I may never find that precise patch of water I fixed my eye on as a child—but it goes on nonetheless. That patch is somewhere in the cycle.

"We must begin thinking like a river if we are to leave a legacy of beauty and life for future generations," said the environmentalist David Brower. A Native American song puts it this way: "The rivers are our sisters, and we must take care of them." In thinking like a river, we reflect on our own lives, our own cycles. In taking care of rivers, we take care of ourselves.

It is our tendency to break the universal cycles (water, the stars, the seasons) into fragments and categorize and name the fragments, so that we lose consciousness of the cycles. "Saranac" means "Place of the red summer," in reference to sumacs, in Algonquian. Are there any sumacs left beside the sweet Saranac's limpid waters? If so, is it because we have taken care of the river? If not, what have we wrought?

In all the world, there is only one river. Water flows in an eternal cycle, and we are part of it. What we do to rivers, we do to ourselves.

Perhaps all of this is why rivers appear in so many of the selections in this anthology. We are part of them, and they of us. As the spiritual puts it, "Give us peace like a river."

ABOUT THE EDITORS

NEAL BURDICK grew up in Plattsburgh, New York, and graduated from St. Lawrence University, where he has been publications writer/editor and an advanced writing instructor since 1977. As a freelance editor and writer, he has published in a variety of genres, from poetry to book reviews, and in a variety of publications, from Fodor's Travel Books to *Blueline*. He even won a short fiction contest once, although he thinks he was the only entrant in his age category. He is editor of *Adirondac*, the magazine of the Adirondack Mountain Club, and a frequent contributor to *Adirondack Explorer* and *Adirondack Life* magazines. Burdick is co-editor,

Tara Freeman.

with Natalia Singer, of the anthology *Living North Country* (North Country Books, 2001) and editor of *The Adirondack Reader, 3rd Ed.* (Adirondack Mountain Club, 2009). He has edited books on the Adirondacks for several regional publishing houses; been a panelist for the New York Foundation for the Arts nonfiction grant program and a commentator on regional writing for the Associated Writing Programs, North Country Public Radio and the Adirondack Park Visitor Interpretive Center; and was for several years a member of the board of directors of the Adirondack Center for Writing. He was a founder and longtime co-director of St. Lawrence's Young Writers Conference.

The author of over thirty collections of poetry and of fiction, Watertown, New York native MAURICE KENNY has been hailed by *World Literature Today* as the dean of Native American poetry. Also an essayist and reviewer, his work appears in nearly one hundred anthologies and textbooks. *The Mama Poems*, an extended elegy, won the American Book Award in 1984 and his books *Between Two Rivers, Blackrobe* and *Isaac Jogues* were nominated for the Pulitzer Prize. However, he considers his most important work to be *Tekonwatonti: Molly Brant, 1735–1795,* a historical poetry journey in many voices that was praised as "a new form of dramatic monologue." He has extended this method in the forthcoming *Conversations with Frida Kahlo: Collage of Memory.* Kenny has been an editor, publisher, arts council panelist and member of the board of directors of the Coordinating Council of Literary Magazines. He has been a visiting professor/poet-in-residence at numerous colleges, including St. Lawrence University, which awarded him an honorary doctorate; the University of Oklahoma; Paul Smith's College; and SUNY Potsdam, where he was writer-in-residence. He was for many years a teaching poet at St. Lawrence's Young Writers Conference.

Phil Gallos.

ABOUT OUR CONTRIBUTORS

Dan Berggren is a tradition-based musician who writes with honesty, humor and a strong sense of place. His songs explore the many dimensions of home and hardworking people, as well as taking care of our planet and each other. A St. Lawrence University graduate, he worked in the woods on forest ranger and survey crews, is professor emeritus of communication at SUNY Fredonia and has released over a dozen albums of fresh, acoustic folk rooted in the Adirondacks.

Jonathan Collier was born in the Schenectady, New York area but grew up in the Adirondacks, outside of Saranac Lake. An avid 4H-er for many years, he still owns a few goats. He DJed for the campus radio station and studied creative writing at SUNY Potsdam. He plans to travel and continue writing as much as possible and would like all to know that goats do not actually eat tin cans.

Tim Fortune is a native of the Adirondacks, which continue to provide him with endless subject matter to paint and showcase the powerful images of nature. After living in various locations and traveling abroad, he and his wife, Diana, returned to Saranac Lake, and in 1994, he opened a studio and gallery in the village's historic downtown. He uses this space not only to display his own art but also as a working studio where visitors and residents can watch him work. He is dedicated to revitalization of the downtown Saranac Lake area through the arts.

RICH FROST grew up in Glens Falls, New York. He graduated from Wesleyan University and Duke University College of Medicine. After completing a residency in internal medicine at the University of Kentucky, he returned north to practice in Plattsburgh, New York. In addition to his medical practice, he has written the travel column "A Day Away," first for the *Chronicle* in Glens Falls and, from 1988 to 2012, for the Sunday *Press-Republican* in Plattsburgh. His fourth book, *Hotel Champlain to Clinton Community College: A Chronicle of Bluff Point*, was published in 2011. He lives in Schuyler Falls, New York, with his wife, Marty, and their yellow Labrador retriever Zoe.

PHIL GALLOS was born in Manhattan, educated in Baltimore and lives in Saranac Lake, New York. He was a reporter, columnist and photographer for the *Adirondack Daily Enterprise*. A founding (and repeating) board member of Historic Saranac Lake (the historic preservation organization), he authored the book *Cure Cottages of Saranac Lake: Architecture and History of a Pioneer Health Resort*. He is a past president of the Arts Council for the Northern Adirondacks, and since 1990 has been a Senior Library Clerk at North Country Community College's Saranac Lake campus. He would tell you that the preceding sentences say nothing about who he is.

EDWARD KANZE is a naturalist, writer and photographer who lives in Bloomingdale, New York, at the edge of the McKenzie Mountain Wilderness. A seventh-generation Adirondacker via his mother, he is also a relative newcomer to the region, having become a full-time resident only in 1999. Ed is the author of seven books, including the acclaimed *Kangaroo Dreaming: An Australian Wildlife Odyssey*. He recently completed a novel about the disappearance of the explorer Henry Hudson and is on the home stretch of a nonfiction book combining personal history, family history and natural history in the Adirondack Mountains.

LITA KELLY spent her elementary and middle school years in Dannemora, New York, and her high school years in Plattsburgh. She earned degrees in both elementary education and reading from SUNY Plattsburgh. As a performing singer/songwriter and guitarist, she found a path into the musical world of rock, folk, blues and country. Working her way through graduate school as a Local Artist in Residence for the Council on the Arts of Clinton County, she taught thousands of fourth-graders their own history through slides, stories and songs. Through two decades as a music teacher at St. John's Academy, Seton Catholic Central and Seton Academy in Plattsburgh, her fascination with local history has accompanied her.

Margaret Olsen was born and raised in Seattle, Washington. She completed her undergraduate degree at St. Lawrence University in 2009, with majors in English and environmental studies. After graduating, she traveled and volunteered on organic farms in New Zealand and hopes to continue writing, traveling and farming in the future.

John Radigan lives in Saranac Lake, New York, and has been on the English/ humanities faculty of Paul Smith's College since 1985. He holds a PhD in English from Syracuse University and an MFA in poetry from Vermont College. His work has appeared in *Blueline*, the Adirondack-themed literary journal, and his poem "Meltwater" was selected for inclusion in *The Blueline Anthology* (Syracuse University Press, 2004) as among the best work to appear in that journal during its first twenty years of publication. He is also an accomplished bagpiper and in 2009 earned a certificate in permaculture design.

North Country Public Radio station manager Ellen Rocco has been with the station since 1980. She has lived on her DeKalb, New York farm since 1971, when she moved to the North Country from New York City. Over the past four decades, she has raised sheep, Percheron horses, chickens, turkeys and a son. She is the producer and host of the contemporary literature series, Readers & Writers on the Air.

Christopher Shaw lived in the Adirondacks for thirty years, working as a caretaker, guide and magazine editor. His essays and stories have appeared in the anthologies *The Nature of Nature*, *The Adirondack Reader* and *Rooted in Rock*, as well as in *Outside*, the *New England Review*, *New York Times* and many other publications. Shaw has received Bread Loaf and New York Foundation for the Arts fellowships. His book *Sacred Monkey River* came out from Norton in 2000. Shaw teaches at Middlebury College and still spends summers with his wife in their cabin on the Saranac River.

Alan Steinberg teaches literature and writing at SUNY Potsdam. He has published fiction (*Cry of the Leopard*, St. Martin's Press; *Divided*, Aegina Press), poetry (*Fathering*, Sarasota Poetry Press; *Ebstein on Reflection*, Idaho State Press) and drama (*The Road to Corinth*, Players Press). His radio play, *The Night Before the Morning After*, won the national award for radio drama sponsored by the American Radio Theatre. Most recently, his play, *The Revision*, won the Nor'easter Playwriting Competition sponsored by the Vermont Actors Repertory Theatre.

JENNIFER DUFFIELD WHITE is a writer, an editor and a student of playing outdoors. She graduated from St. Lawrence University and later spent seven lovely years living in the Adirondacks. Her writing has appeared in publications such as *Adirondack Life*, *Women's Adventure*, *Terrain.org*, *Narrative Magazine* and *Witness*. She lives in Missoula, Montana, and has an MFA in creative writing from the University of Montana.

ABOUT OUR ILLUSTRATORS

In addition to those named here, writers Dan Berggren and Tim Fortune, whose biographies appear above, also contributed illustrations.

JIM BULLARD is an artist/photographer living in the North Country of New York, north and west of the Adirondack Park. His photography consists primarily of landscapes and flowers. He has a blog at http://jims-ramblings.blogspot.com and photo galleries at http://jimbullard.zenfolio.com.

MATT CARPENTER was an assistant to the St. Lawrence University Photographer before graduating from St. Lawrence with a biology major in 2010. Also a volunteer member of the local fire and rescue company while in college, he is an EMT with a private ambulance service in Oxford, Maine.

TARA FREEMAN has been the university photographer at St. Lawrence University since 2000. She has seventeen years of experience as a professional photographer. Before coming to St. Lawrence, she was a staff photographer at the *Olean Times Herald*, in Olean, New York.

A 1970 graduate of Gloversville (New York) High School and a 1976 graduate of St. Lawrence University, BRIAN HENRY has had his bird photos published in, among others, *Adirondack Life, Birder's World, Bird Watcher's Digest, Time Magazine, WildBird* and many birding field guides. Retired from the New York State Thruway Authority/Canal Corporation, he works part-time as a health insurance navigator for the Family Counseling Center of Fulton County (New York), Inc.

LIZ HUBBARD graduated from St. Lawrence University in 2003 and owns her own photography business, Willow Tree Images, in Potsdam, New York. She specializes in portrait and lifestyle photography. Her website is www.willowtreeimages.com.

Born in Chicago and raised in Connecticut, DEBBIE KANZE moved to Saranac Lake in the Adirondacks in 1999. A photographer by passion and avocation, she serves as activities director at Saranac Village at Will Rogers, a senior independent living residence in Saranac Lake. Nature, landscapes and intriguing patterns of light and shadow on water are favorite subjects for her camera.

For more than 25 years, MARK KURTZ has been providing Saranac Lake, Lake Placid and the Adirondack region with fine art, commercial, and wedding photography. He received a BFA from Alfred University and has taught photography in high school, college, and workshop environments. A founding member of the Adirondack Artists' Guild, he is widely recognized as one of the Adirondack region's preeminent artists. He is a regular contributing photographer to *Adirondack Life* magazine and his work has been featured in *Skiing* magazine and in countless advertisements and annual reports for regional and national clients.

BARRY LOBDELL lives in Saranac Lake, in the heart of the Adirondack Park. His photography centers around the mountains and waterways that surround him, as well as other landscapes in the United States, England and Canada. He is a member of the Adirondack Artists Guild, and his work is held in many private and public collections. His photographs have been honored in both national and regional competitions and have been published in many forms throughout his career.

DEB MACKENZIE is a devoted mother of three children. She conducts groundbreaking research in radiology, primarily neuro-modalities (CT and MRI). Her hobbies include studying wildlife, travel, photography, baking and numerous outdoor activities. She and her husband, Kevin (below), are official photographers for the Adirondack Wildlife and Rehabilitation

Center as well as freelance photographers in the Lake Placid, New York area, where they reside.

Kevin "MudRat" MacKenzie is assistant registrar at St. Lawrence University as well as an Adirondack writer and photographer. He is an avid outdoorsman whose passion is exploring the backcountry of the Adirondacks in all seasons. For further information and photographs, visit www.mackenziefamily.com/46/46r.html or www.mackenziefamily.com/creativenature.

Jessica Riehl is an environmental photographer who lives in Oregon. She grew up on a sheep farm, was a U.S. Navy officer, has worked in the recycling industry, majored in environmental science at Oregon State University and has studied toward her master's degree in environmental science and policy at Johns Hopkins University.

Photographer and writer Betsy Tisdale's work has appeared in the Plattsburgh *Press Republican*, *Adirondack Life*, *The Conservationist* and *Adirondac* (the magazine of the Adirondack Mountain Club), and she contributed a chapter to the anthology *Living North Country* (North Country Books, 2001). A resident of Potsdam, New York, she is the author of a chapter on Amish farming practices in this book's companion volume, *North Country Reflections: On Life and Living in the Foothills and the Valleys.*

Henning Vahlenkamp works in information technology in the telecommunications industry. He has been exploring and photographing the Adirondacks in his spare time for fifteen years. An Adirondack Mountain Club (ADK) member for nearly as long, his photos have appeared in various ADK publications.

Eric and Jean Williams-Bergen have been homesteading on their land near Canton, New York, since 1999. Their lovely goats supply their family with milk that they use fresh as well as make into yogurt, soft cheeses and goat milk soap. In addition to the goats, they raise chickens, rabbits, dogs and cats, two ponies and the occasional pair of sheep. Their garden supplies all of their vegetables for their family as well as their goats, who eat large quantities of cabbage, beets and squash each winter.